This book will help any [...] just starting out or have been i[...] refocuses your work back to the basics. Work smarter, not harder! Being thoughtful around the details and consistent with your messaging will absolutely lead to greater dollars raised. All the steps are laid out brilliantly.

(**Jennifer Steffus,** Chief Development Officer, National Safety Council)

What a gift to the sector, particularly as so many organizations build back stronger. The Process-Driven Annual Fund is an easy page-turning must read for savvy development professionals seeking to take their annual giving program to the next level. This book provides proven and new approaches to building and accelerating unstoppable momentum in your fundraising program. Give your annual fund program some tender loving care, as Ron recommends, and watch your donors fall in love with your organization for life. Looking forward to seeing The Process-Driven Annual Fund on every development professional's desk!

(**Brenda B. Asare,** President & CEO, The Alford Group)

__The Process-Driven Annual Fund__ provides an inspirational introduction to the annual fund process. While recognizing the importance of donor-centered relationships, the book details *the components essential to building a successful annual fund through direct mail. Through years of professional trials and triumphs, the author addresses the wide range of topics contributing to a thriving annual fund.*

(**John Andreasan**, Associate Development Director, Anne Carlsen Center Foundation)

Fundraising is an art. The art of compelling storytelling. Ron has created a compelling story for building a successful annual fund. He makes an easy case and provides you with a summary at the end of each chapter. Ron remains the educator and brings that into focus - write about the heroes of your organization, solve challenges, and create the pipeline for donor giving. I especially appreciated his focus that appeals can be personalized, donor centered, compelling - and then adding your unexpected gift of appreciation to the donor that builds relationships with deep roots - building a culture of philanthropy. Well done, Ron. You and Sue have built a great business - integrity and fun - by listening and building relationships with your partners - thanks for putting that knowledge and adding your personal touch to each chapter - family - in this book.

(**David J. Eaton MA**, Director of Development, Office of Medical Advancement, University of Illinois College of Medicine)

What others are saying:

- *Practical, no-nonsense guidance. This book lays out a fantastic pathway toward Annual Fund success.*
- *Such a great reminder of how critical Annual Fund efforts are for non-profit fundraising! This book provides great reminders for us long-tome fundraisers to refocus on as well as a thoughtful path for success for those just getting into the industry.*
- *Tried and true practical stories and applications to improve your annual fund efforts from experts who have been in the trenches with us fundraisers for more than 30 years! True partners in fundraising!*

THE PROCESS-DRIVEN ANNUAL FUND

For more information please visit www.ronrescigno.com

Published by Fig Factor Media, LLC | www.figfactormedia.com

Printed in the United States of America

ISBN: 978-1-952779-06-0
Library of Congress Control Number: 2020913807

THE PROCESS-DRIVEN ANNUAL FUND

Turn your Annual Fund Campaign INTO A Revenue Machine

RON RESCIGNO

To all those who have chosen fundraising as their profession and dedicate themselves to fulfilling the vision and mission of nonprofit organizations worldwide—you make the world a better place--and for that, I salute you!

Acknowledgements

In many ways, this book is a summation of the work I've done with nonprofit organizations over the past 28 years. Upon reflection, I worked for nonprofit educational institutions for 23 years beginning back in 1971. So many good causes.

My book, **The Process-Driven Annual Fund**, is not solely my brainchild. It belongs to others whose words echo in my ears even today, *"You know, you really should write a book."* I am grateful to them all. I may not remember them all, but I want to thank each and every one of them.

This book would not have happened without the love and support of my wife and business partner, Sue, who is also the president of Rescigno's Fundraising Professionals.

Plain and simple, she is the one who truly made me believe I had a book in me. She's never let me settle for less than my best in myself and has always seen in me what I couldn't or refused to see in myself. I'm beyond grateful to her for the work she personally put into this book. Whether it was bringing order to the sometimes-chaotic nature of my writing style, or creating a table of contents or simply making sure that every "t" was crossed and "i" dotted, she was there to provide what I needed. Sue, I love you. Thanks for helping me to become more than I thought I ever could be.

And special recognition also goes to my son, Dominic, for his book cover design and continuous words of encouragement. When your son tells you, *"You should, dad, you really should,"* well, you do. I hope him seeing me write this book, in some small way, inspired him to write the screen play he's currently working on.

And to my daughter, Jessie, now a project manager at Rescigno's, a heartfelt thank you for being the kind, warm-hearted person who constantly reminds me of what's good about being alive.

This world is a better place because of the people who you meet in nonprofit fundraising. People just like you, I'm sure. And because of the nature of the work required of fundraising professionals, you certainly get all my respect and admiration.

There is little respect or recognition for those who inspire donors to give at initial levels that place them at the bottom of the so-called donor pyramid. However, make no mistake, without the work you, the annual fund director; you, the writer of the inspiring story; or you, the data entry person does at this level, there would be very few, if any, major donor prospects to cultivate, much less anyone interested in planned giving. You also have all my respect. It's unglamorous work you do, but so very necessary.

While my mom, Mary, and Sue's mom, Frances, were alive, they were such a big part of our business. I know they'd be proud that I wrote this book. Two bigger cheerleaders could never be found. They know how I feel, but I want to acknowledge that appreciation publicly.

A special thanks for their personal contributions to this

book go to George Boodrookas, executive director at Modesto Jr. College Foundation in Modesto, California; Diana Pollard, executive director at Dutchess Community College Foundation, Poughkeepsie, New York; Eric Wilke, chief advancement officer at the Anne Carlsen Center in Fargo, North Dakota; Sandra Wilcoxon, executive director at Recovery International in Oakbrook, Illinois; Kate Bousum, chief advancement officer at Child's Voice in Wood Dale, Illinois; Mary Ellen O'Neill, chief advancement officer at Bishop Noll High School in Hammond, Indiana; and Kathi Barth, development director at Sisters of the Holy Family of Nazareth. I believe your stories are priceless!

I feel very grateful for having met certain people who acted as mentors for me (and most of them didn't even know it): Leon Clarin, who taught me the wisdom behind the words, *"Start with the low-hanging fruit,"* when we purchased our first digital press and Leo Raymond, head man at Mailer's Hub. Leo knows more about USPS regulations, and is able to explain them in down-to-earth English better than anyone I know. He could probably do it in Italian, even though he's not one. John Foley, aka Smarty-britches from Grow Socially and Interlink One, who early on encouraged us to add social media as part of our services. Joe Langenderfer, now the executive director at the diocese of Raleigh-Durham and formerly of the Joliet Diocese. Joe couldn't believe it when Sue advised him to "Mail less, but make sure you're mailing to the right people." He said, "You mean I'll get a better ROI if I ask less people?" And, he raised more money that year than he did the previous year with a larger list!

A very special thank you goes out to the publisher, Jacqueline Ruiz, at Fig Factor Media and her team. Without them, I don't know if I would have been able to complete this book. Jackie's thoughtful and positive attitude were always a bright spot on days when I needed it most.

I'm sure there are many others I should be thanking, but if I mentioned everyone, my acknowledgment section would be longer than my book! Please know I certainly appreciate all of you as well.

FOREWORD
BY: SUE RESCIGNO

It is with much pride and gratitude that I sit down to write this Foreword for Ron's book. I am Ron's wife of 31 years, and business partner for 28 years which makes me uniquely qualified to introduce you to Ron both personally and professionally. When we met, I was a director of development and Ron was a principal of a high school. Neither of us knew at the time what a journey God had planned for us. Ron is the steady to my storm. He is the rock of both the family and the business. Ron and I have been through so many things together and he is that guy, the guy that I can look to across a crowded room, and with a simple nod to each other, we know that we've got this, whatever life throws our way. Whether it's a family crisis or a business crisis, Ron always shows up.

Ron does the same thing with the many non-profits that he works with every day. He is an expert in annual fund. He is their resource on their fundraising appeals, newsletters, impact reports, etc. He helps them craft their messages and he pushes them forward to expand their annual fund programs. He is always at the forefront of what's new and exciting in fundraising and communications. Ron, in an effort to help nonprofits, has learned more about communicating with donors and prospects than anyone I know. He is constantly researching and reaching out to clients with pertinent information that they can use in their planning and fundraising strategies.

I have made a lifetime career of fundraising, specifically annual fund, and what Ron has compiled in his book, *The Process-Driven Annual Fund, Turn Your Annual Fund Campaign Into a Revenue Machine,* is gold. He has taken years of practical research and study that has proven successful time after time and created a proven process. The truth is, if you follow this process, your annual fund results will improve—guaranteed! The key is to follow all the steps that Ron has detailed for you and your annual fund will provide you a pipeline of donors for years to come. I wish I had a book like this when I started my career.

Contents

Introduction

In February of 2020, I thought I was finished writing this book. I really did. This is a project I'd been working on for several years and I had certainly grown tired of well-meaning people asking me when the book was coming out.

It's funny how the best laid plans can be altered, seemingly at a moment's notice.

That's when March 2020 happened. So, I'm writing now about the devastating effects of the Coronavirus Pandemic and how it has affected nonprofits and their ability to continue to raise much needed funds for those their missions serve.

At Rescigno's, we were able to call upon our past experiences in order to advise our clients on what they should be doing as the crisis began to unfold.

The medical experts were predicting that the next several months were going to be bad. They were right. As mid-April turned into May, there was a frightening spike in confirmed cases and, unfortunately, deaths from COVID-19.

Fundraising during a crisis is challenging, but we know that people, historically, will continue to give. This especially goes for an organization's most loyal and best performing donors. We also know that donors want to give and help. They simply need to be presented with the opportunity to make a difference in the lives of real people.

We believe that staying the course is very important when

it comes to communicating both needs and opportunities to donors, especially during a crisis. And unlike during the Great Recession (2008-09), when nonprofits froze almost all fundraising/marketing spending, nonprofits continued to communicate with their donors and continued to ask for and receive support.

Back to the matter at hand–the annual fund. If you're a development director, an executive director, a board member of a non-profit organization or someone who's involved in building an annual fund program, this book is for you. I don't say that with any sense of entitlement, and I'm certainly not bragging. But I have learned that there is a process involved in making the annual fund successful, and I am excited to share that knowledge with you.

If you're asking yourself who is this Ron Rescigno guy, and why does he think he's qualified to write a book about the annual fund, I don't blame you.

Since 1992, it's been my privilege and honor to work alongside my wife, Sue, in this adventure we've been on. Over that period of time, I've immersed myself in what it takes for organizations to have success with annual giving. Sue's the one with professional fundraising training. I learned so much from her and then just filled in the blanks as I went along.

Whether it's data analysis, donor retention, letter writing, copy editing, new donor welcome strategies or any number of annual appeal topics, I've learned that sticking to the process leads to success.

You see, we truly believe that the annual fund and fundraising in general, is a Process-Driven Discipline and that if you follow tried-and-true, time-tested annual fund practices, you can't lose. That's not to say that there aren't bumps along the way. There are—always. But when you apply the principles I'm about to share here in The Process-Driven Annual Fund to your fundraising program, those bumps become less frequent and less painful.

During the course of this book, I will show you how following the process makes everything easier.

Ahh! The annual fund. Habit forming, tried and true, and a dependable source of income, some say. Others have lambasted it as a pain in the neck, annoying, groveling for pennies, and below their dignity.

Whatever! Here's what I believe:

Without consistent annual giving and without investing in it, your nonprofit organization will be challenged to ever grow revenue or its overall fundraising program.

Is it possible to have a successful fundraising campaign without an annual fund? I suppose so. Is it likely to succeed for any length of time? Highly unlikely. In fact, I've never encountered it.

The organizations that invest in and follow through on well-thought out and executed annual fund plans will thrive.

By paying special attention to the same rules used in the for-profit world, nonprofits and their causes can and will succeed. However, there are a few obstacles that must be faced head on.

Nonprofits must understand and be willing to talk about the need for investing in the tools that lead to annual fund success. Your donors and your boards must be made to understand that development work, the work you do, comes with a price tag attached. That's about as bluntly as I can say it. Stop cowering in a corner when the subject of cost comes up in conversations. You have nothing to be ashamed of. Boards and donors need to be educated that without investing, you'll never grow your program, and you'll never increase revenue, not just for the annual fund, but for your entire advancement program.

I'm not sure when this started, but there is a very erroneous way of thinking that says doing good and doing well financially can't co-exist. I'm fairly certain you'll agree with me, especially when you consider the disparity between what a nonprofit CEO earns when compared to his for-profit counterparts. Think about it for a minute—isn't the impact of nonprofit CEOs on society and the economy just as powerful? Even more so, if you ask me.

For-profit organizations seldom, if ever, are investigated for spending on the advertising and marketing they do. On the contrary, it's a given. Now think of your own organization and how often it is criticized for frivolous spending. Has this happened at your place? I'd be surprised if it hasn't. If you're a customer of a particular brand, say Dr. Pepper soda pop, you really don't give two hoots how much they spend on advertising or marketing their product. Agreed? Why then, do donors and boards, and the public, get so offended when a nonprofit like yours spends money on advertising and marketing, even when you can prove that doing so makes you even more effective?

Plain and simple, at Rescigno's we've developed The Process-Driven Annual Fund, and it works. More on that coming up.

If you walk away with nothing else from reading these pages, please know this: You should be continuing to communicate with your donors. Do more, not less. Your donors, both your best and most loyal, want and need to help you during an emergency and at regular intervals throughout any given year. They want to be a part of the difference you are making every day.

Ron Rescigno
May 2020

HERE'S A GREAT EXAMPLE of CONTINUING TO COMMUNICATE WITH YOUR DONORS DURING A CRISIS FROM ONE OF OUR CURRENT CLIENTS!

We had just wrapped up our Annual Appeal on 6/30/20. The Annual Fund goal (unrestricted funds) was $315,000 vs. $289,000 in 2019. We came in at $314,500 in a pretty difficult economy. In April we were forced to cancel our spring scholarship event where we need to raise $40,000-$50,000 for current year student scholarships. We took a chance on a virtual auction in late May using the GiveSmart platform and a live stream on the final evening. We were blown away by the support we received from our constituents, raising over $72,000! Finally, we held our Alumni & Friends Golf Outing yesterday, unsure of how many would attend. We had the same number of golfers as last year and a slight uptick in sponsorships...so we did well. I always remember Ron's advice--even in tough economic times, keeping lines of communication open with our constituents is critical. It worked! A number of our key donors came through with second gifts for the Annual Fund and even additional gifts for tuition assistance for families who lost jobs. So, while a crazy year, it was also very gratifying.

Mary Ellen O'Neill
Director of Advancement
Bishop Noll Institute

CHAPTER 1

THE JOURNEY BEGINS
First, a love story

Sue and I met at Josephinum High School in the Wicker Park area of Chicago in 1985. She came to "The Jo" from St. Ignatius Academy, where she had started her professional career.

I can remember, like it was yesterday, the day Sue, my business partner and my love, got the idea for opening up her own business. Little did I know how much it would change my life, and that of so many other people.

Sue was the director of development at Mt. Assisi Academy in Lemont, Illinois, back in 1992. Sadly, Mt. Assisi is no longer in operation. At that time, however, it was an all-girls' Catholic high school in the southwest suburbs of Chicago. I was the dean of students and director of recruitment.

Sue and the principal of Mt. Assisi, Sr. Denise, were going on a visit to a major gift prospect whose two daughters had graduated from the school. Coincidentally, he owned a direct mail house.

I have to admit that I had only a passing knowledge of direct mail, much less a direct-mail house. Anyway, Sue and Sr. Denise came back from their visit and shared with me how the conversation with this wealthy prospect went.

As we talked, Sue said that she had gotten an idea while she was there. You have to understand that Sue, unlike me, comes from an entrepreneurial family. Her maiden name, Krapil, is famous pretty much anywhere you go south of Madison St. in Chicago and surrounding suburbs. Her dad owned Krapil's, the Great Steak, on 111th St. in Worth, Illinois, for years. The steaks WERE great, believe me.

Let me just say this about my life with my beautiful Sue. I was 36 when I met her. Thirty-six—yet my life began the day we met. No lie. What's that funny quote from Friends that Phoebe once used? "He's her lobster!" The point is that she's my lobster. She's really the reason for me writing this book.

To this day, I know enough to know that when Sue has an idea for something it could mean trouble, or, in this case, opportunity. She explained to me what a direct mail house was and then asked me a pivotal question.

Sue: "Why couldn't we do that?"

Me: "Do what?"

Sue: "Open up a direct mail house?"

Me: "Where?"

Sue: "In our garage."

Me: "How?"

Sue: "I've got a plan."

Me: "Why would we do this?"

Sue: "Because we want to be our own bosses, don't we?"

Me: "I guess so, but why would anyone want to trust us with their mail?"

Sue: "Because they would know that I would take care of their mailings and we know so many people at other schools who like and respect us, that's why!"

Me: "When do you want to do this?"

Sue: "I'll get back to you on that, but soon!"

Since then, and even before, I've always said that living with Sue is like living with Lucy Ricardo from the old "I Love Lucy" show. And as she knows, I mean that in only the most loving of ways.

Sue followed her dream to be an entrepreneur, and I went along for the ride. And what a ride it's been—in life and in business!

From 1992 to 1997, we ran what was then Rescigno's Rapid Mailing Service from a two-car garage in Evergreen Park, Illinois. From 1997-2001, we worked from another two-car garage in Oak Lawn.

You might be thinking, garage? Yuck! On the contrary, both garages were the envy of those neighborhoods. They were heated, air conditioned, carpeted, paneled, insulated, and furnished with the best ceiling lights I could find.

There used to be so much activity in and out of our garage in Oak Lawn that we were once accused of running a bookie joint. I kid you not.

A nosy, or to be kind, "concerned" neighbor had reported to the village that there were constant truck deliveries to our driveway. When you're doing a 20,000-piece direct mail project, it's going to require about 40 or 50 boxes worth of stationery, reply devices and envelopes.

Come to think of it, I guess the same would apply if I was having parlay cards printed up and delivered too. That's what the nosy neighbor suggested was going on in our garage. Maybe because my last name is Rescigno!

Luckily, our neighbor on the other side of us was an Oak Lawn policeman, also Italian. He took us to City Hall, made sure we had all the proper papers for a business license and told them we were good people who weren't up to any funny business.

Back then, we were pretty much just a mail house. We would laser-print personalized letters, address envelopes, and manually sort the addresses for the post office. We'd apply pressure sensitive labels from a mail machine that a friend of Sue's, who worked for one of our first clients, Marist High School, had given her.

Then we'd stuff the envelopes with the letters and other pieces, get out the wet sponges, and seal the envelopes. I would get home from my day job and load the work that was ready for delivery to the post office into our family van.

We knew the time had come to get the business out of the house when we found out that our daughter thought her last name was Rescigno's Rapid Mailing Service. No, I'm not kidding. During the hours of 9 - 5 we answered the phone by saying, "Rescigno's Rapid Mailing Service, may I help you?"

In 1999, our daughter, Jessie, then four-years-old, was sitting at the kitchen table late one afternoon signing Valentine cards as Sue was preparing dinner. At that time, she knew how to write her name but she was taking so long with each card that Sue went over to her to see what she was doing. She was clearly writing her name but then scribbling some words after Rescigno. After a long while, Sue finally asked,

"Jess, what are you writing that's taking so long?"

Jessie answered, "I'm writing my name, mommy!"

"My goodness," Sue said, "I can see Jessie Rescigno but what are those other words."

Finally, Jessie looked up at Sue and said proudly, "Mommy, that's the rest of our name. See, it says Jessie Rescigno's Rapid Mailing Service."

Out of the mouths of babes!!

We worked out of our garage until 2001. As time went on, we were picking up more clients through word of mouth, which is, by far, the best kind of advertising you could ever ask for.

A competitor of ours once said we were the "Marshall Field of direct mail." If you're young enough, you may not know about Marshall Field, but that's quite a compliment. Marshall Field was a very famous and beloved department store in downtown Chicago and several other locations that ceased operations in 2005. The store was known for its "exceptional level of quality and customer service." We're very proud of that unsolicited testimony.

While the picture I paint here seems mostly rosy, dark, frightful days were ahead of us as the 2000s loomed.

First, there was the ripple effect of the terrible 9-11 attacks on our nation. Slowly, but surely, the aftermath of those days did have an effect on the economy as it trickled its way down to the nonprofit sector, our sweet spot.

Budgets were being cut, many drastically. Clients were slashing their mailing lists. Some stopped communicating with prospects and only concentrated on donors. The problem here is that a nonprofit cannot sustain its fundraising program without continually prospecting for new donors.

An organization like Rescigno's can preach until it's blue in the face that the last thing a nonprofit should do in times of economic distress is cut its marketing budget, but for many of our nonprofit clients, it was the first thing they did.

Then there was 2008. It was the beginning of the great recession and donations to nearly every charitable organization faltered, according to Giving USA. So much so that it was the steepest downfall in our country's history, dropping by 5.7 percent.

The economy had been the focus of many headlines from 2007-2012. Most people outside the nonprofit world didn't consider the impact of the ups and downs of the economy on charitable organizations.

By the time October of 2012 rolled around, more than 50 percent of nonprofits reported **no increase in giving** during the first three quarters of the year. In December of the same year, Philanthropy.com noted that during the recession, giving among upper-income Americans declined by $30 billion. It was also reported that individuals earning less than $100,000 decreased their giving by as much as $4 billion.

Actually, by the end of 2010, the economic free fall had started to adjust itself, thank God. But the ramifications were felt long after that. You know how it is when you go sledding down a hill. Going down is fast and exhilarating. The climb back up, however, is not nearly so fast, and certainly nowhere near as much fun. By the time you climb back up the hill toting your sled, you're tired, right?

Likewise, Rescigno's was hanging on, but barely. Sue and I had a critical decision to make. We had lost nearly two-thirds of our business in 2008, and knew that we had to change with the times.

We'd just been putting off what we knew we needed to do and should have done long ago.

We were ready.

As often happens in life, however, fate had other plans for us.

A Real Wake-Up Call

We were on a family vacation in Disney World to celebrate the graduation of our son, Dominic, from high school, and Jessie's graduation from grammar school, when Guillian-Barre Syndrome almost took me out for good.

Guillian-Barre is a debilitating syndrome in which the body's immune system attacks the central-nervous system. In short, a paralytic disease that can, and will, kill you if not treated.

Sparing you most of the gory details--over the course of a three-day period, I went from feeling a tingling around my neck, to a tightness around my spine, to being paralyzed from the neck down. After spending a week in critical intensive care, and another week in the hospital, I was released in a wheel chair.

Talk about a wake-up call.

Anyway, I was in a wheelchair, or needed a walker, for the better part of six months. I had to learn to walk again. The rehab was so much fun and games that I had to have steroids prescribed for the pain of getting my muscles to function again. Basically, I had to re-learn how to use them. As a result of the steroids, I gained 30 pounds.

By late September I was able to walk, slowly, unaided again.

Finally, in November, I was able to get back to Rescigno's. Thank God Sue had kept the place going. She's always been the star of this show anyway.

The problem was that I was our salesperson, so for the six months I was out, there were no new sales going on. Anyone who's ever neglected doing new donor acquisition knows that when you miss acquiring new donors for that length of time there's going to be a gap in revenue. The same applies to business. You have to work on retaining and prospecting at the same time.

This was the perfect storm of events for Rescigno's. Our fortitude was tested to its very core because, as I mentioned, we had already lost two-thirds of our business (due to the recession) with no new business coming in.

What to do?

We could say that it had been a nice run and give up. And at times, both Sue and I had convinced ourselves that it was time to start looking for employment outside of Rescigno's.

I could still probably have gotten a job in a school. I was 57 at the time, and though that's not the age that most schools are looking to hire someone, I had a great track record of experience to bring to an educational institution in any of a number of capacities. As for Sue, we both were fairly confident she could land on her feet at a nonprofit somewhere as a Vice President of Advancement or Executive Director.

But that's not the course we chose.

The turning point came when we were approached by others who smelled blood in the water and offered us a dime for every dollar the business was worth.

I was so angry at these offers that I didn't give Sue much of a chance to think about them. I know what you're thinking. *Ron, it's not personal, it's just business.* Anyway, I said "no" very firmly.

One day we met with a guy I called 'The Angel of Death.' Now, you've got to picture him—black suit and pants, black knit shirt and black suede loafers. Those suede loafers did me in. Back in the day in my old neighborhood…well, I'll leave the rest to your imagination.

Everybody needs motivation of one kind or another. Some respond to positive motivation, others to negative. I guess I respond positively to negative motivation, if that makes sense.

This guy predicted that we'd be out of business within a year. Hearing those words come out of his mouth and looking at this modern-day Captain of Doom was just the kick-in-the-butt motivation I needed. He was looking to purchase our company and offered us the aforementioned dime-on-the-dollar.

Poor Sue. Talk about being beaten up. The bank was putting us through hell too. They were going to foreclose on our mortgage for the office building, not because of any missed payments but because the bank that we had the loan with had failed and the new bank didn't want our mortgage. Did you know banks could do that? Neither did I! I guess that story could be another book!

Anyway, I looked at Mr. Angel of Death and said "no way," and led him unceremoniously out the door. Then I looked at Sue, usually the most positive, strong, and upbeat of people. For once, it was my turn to cheerlead.

I said to Sue, *"We are not going to let anyone low ball all the hard and good work we've done for our clients over the years. We're going to figure out what we have to do to build the business back up. Whatever it takes, we'll do it."*

In the end, those offers did more than just anger us. They emboldened us. But we were still in the same dilemma. How were we going to build the business back up? We had to find a way.

I once heard inspirational speaker, Zig Ziglar, say, *"Success occurs when opportunity meets preparation."*

I guess, unknowingly, Sue and I had been preparing for this moment for a very long time.

As I mentioned just a moment ago, the answer had been staring us in the face for years.

TAKING ACTION CREATES OPPORTUNITIES

Like nonprofit organizations that say they want to raise more money, saying and doing are two very different things.

I believe that nonprofits really do want to raise more money than they currently raise. Who doesn't? **The problem is, doing what's necessary to change an organization's way of doing things isn't that easy.**

It's like losing weight, isn't it? Every year people say they're going to commit to losing weight. They invest lots of money in health club memberships and weight loss programs, but when it comes right down to exercising or pushing the plate away, well, that's hard to do. Especially when your options are carrot cake or a Sicilian cannoli.

Nonprofits changing their behavior usually implies going from an organization-centered frame of mind to a donor-centered approach. It takes work, perseverance, and a willingness to change an organization's entire culture.

The same went for Rescigno's. We had been outsourcing hundreds of thousands of dollars in printing each year to printers who would "do their thing" before sending us back the materials they had printed. We would then do the mail house portion of the job–stuff, seal, sort, bundle, etc. in preparation for delivery to the post office.

Thankfully, Sue had done the research while I was sick. I had been doing some thinking myself. We needed to keep the print portion of the work in house--keep those hundreds of thousands of dollars instead of giving it to outside printers.

Remember what I said about opportunity meeting preparation?

To say this was a major gamble on our part is to state the obvious. That new printer I mentioned was about the cost of a nice three-bedroom home in the suburbs. No lie.

All's fair in love and war, I guess. And make no mistake, this was a war we were waging—a struggle for our very existence.

We decided to go "all in" and purchased a digital press which allowed us to do personalized, segmented versions of letters to our clients' donors and prospects which, we knew, would be the key to direct mail and annual fund success. Our clients needed to start segmenting and targeting their mail, and with the digital press we would be able to help them.

In 2010, we did it! We invested in a printer that would allow us to offer our clients the ability to send different versions of the same letter to their various donor and nondonor segments.

It was time to *go after the low-hanging fruit*. In other words, talk to our current customers before going after new prospects. We were able to show our nonprofit clients what this new variable, digital technology, could do for their program. Once we did, we were off and running once again.

Ultimately, taking action led to new opportunities. During this time, when we talked with our clients, we discovered that because of budget cuts, they needed help with planning, budgeting, and analyzing their programs. What followed was the adventure of a lifetime, and one where we learned the repeatable success of the **Process-Driven Annual Fund.**

Things to Remember:

- Come what may, if you're not reaching out to your donors and prospects to explain to them why their gifts are essential and how it will make the world a better place, even if only for one person, you will not receive the support you need to fulfill your mission.

- An annual fund that is **Process Driven** will bring in the revenue needed for your organization to build a following of loyal, recurring donors.

CHAPTER 2

THE PROCESS-DRIVEN APPROACH: A NEW WAY TO LOOK AT THE ANNUAL FUND

The annual fund is nothing new—or is it? As you will see, the annual fund is anything but annual. It is, however, one of the most cost-effective ways for you to find new donors.

When I stop to think about it, Sue and I are similar to matchmakers in that we enjoy helping nonprofit professionals find and cultivate long-lasting relationships with donors.

As annual fund consultants, **what we hope to do is facilitate loving relationships that connect hearts and minds to causes.** When this happens, voila! The money follows.

We have realized over the past 28 years that there is a definite process to raising more money and finding new donors for the annual fund. Therefore, we have developed the **Process-Driven Annual Fund** that has proven successful year after year, client after client. Following it, in order, enables nonprofits to create a solid annual fund which establishes a long-term habit of giving.

If you use the content described in this book, I'm certain you'll be better able to engage your donors in more emotional heartfelt ways, and that the end result will be both stronger relationships with your donors that endure the test of time, and much more revenue than you ever thought possible.

So, let's begin with an overview of the steps in **The Process-Driven Annual Fund** before we delve into each one individually.

DISCOVERY

In this first step, you should examine what is currently being done in your annual fund. Is there a written plan, or is it all in your head? Is there a calendar that is currently being followed? What communication is currently happening with your prospects and donors? Are you soliciting your donors and how often? Are you analyzing the results of those appeals? When was the last time you analyzed your database? How are donors being acknowledged, and what are you doing to keep your donors? Always examine and evaluate the current program before you make any changes.

DATA WEALTH SCREENING, ANALYTICS, DONOR PROFILING

Know who you are mailing to and why. Wealth screenings help nonprofit organizations forecast future donor behavior. These screenings offer an overview of a prospect's giving future as it considers such things as past giving, involvement with other nonprofits, any owned real estate, as well as other factors that, when studied as a whole, allow for predictive donor profiles. It's during this process that philanthropic indicators come to light, as well. This step aims to answer one essential question: what is the giving potential of any one prospect? Donor profiling creates a snapshot of your typical donor. This will help you find new donors.

PLANNING, MESSAGING AND SEGMENTATION

If you want to be successful with your annual fund you must have a plan in place to communicate with your donors. Having a written plan makes it easier to identify program goals while listing tactics, messaging by audience, and timing of pieces. It's the plan that provides structure and focus, and ultimately creates the habit of giving because your donors and prospects rely on that communication from your organization.

ACKNOWLEDGEMENT PROGRAM

When donors make a gift in response to an ask, they have made an emotional decision. They feel good about having supported a cause they believe in. Your acknowledgement, the way you thank them, is essential to keeping those good feelings going. A good acknowledgement program shows donors that their gift mattered, that they are appreciated, and how their support is helping to fulfill your mission. If your acknowledgements are boring, you will miss out on opportunities to connect on a deeper level with your donors.

DONOR LOYALTY AND RETENTION

You probably already know that over one-half of all first-time donors never make a second gift. The first step to improving retention is to maintain donor loyalty. Understanding donor motivation, communicating with them, recognizing their support, stewarding their gifts, and engaging with them are all steps that lead to greater donor loyalty and, ultimately, donor retention.

RESULTS ANALYSIS

When it comes to studying and reporting on how your annual fund is performing, you need to ask hard questions like, *"Is one kind of appeal doing better than another kind, and can the language or messaging in the appeal be improved?"* Neglecting to thoroughly measure and analyze your appeal results means you'll likely miss critical information that would have helped you raise more money on your next appeal.

THINGS TO REMEMBER:

- Just as there is a process involved in building a romantic relationship, there is also a very similar process involved in cultivating long-lasting relationships with donors.
- You must have an annual fund plan that has been well-thought out and describes goals and tactics to be used.
- Your plan must be in writing so that it can be reviewed periodically.

CHAPTER 3

DIRECT MAIL REMAINS THE #1 SOURCE FOR ANNUAL GIFTS

Before we start expanding on the processes, let's get a few things straight. Direct mail still remains the #1 source of finding and retaining your donors.

Sue and I were in Hawaii, attending a mailers' conference in February of 2007. It seems like a lifetime ago.

On the first day of the conference, we were attending a session on the future of direct mail when the speaker started out by warning the attendees that they had better get their business affairs in order—quickly. In his opinion, a recession was coming and soon. What a buzzkill. What was wrong with this guy? We weren't prepared, or in a mood to hear that.

Many mailers that were there enjoying the nice weather and the ambience are no longer around. Sad, but true. The speaker said that the internet and email were quickly making mail obsolete and soon direct mail would be gone forever.

Here we were in paradise and we felt like he had just sucker punched us in the gut. One man stood up and said, "You came all the way to Hawaii to tell us that? Thanks a lot. "

As it turns out, he was only partially correct.

Sue and I took some comfort in the fact that we had a niche that we hoped and believed would survive the coming rough times. We just didn't know how rough. We've lived with this threat for some time though.

The so-called "experts" have been predicting the death of printed direct mail since the start of the internet. Talk about dying a slow death! It's been such a slow death that a cure was found: highly personalized, *segmented direct mail*.

Production costs, postage rate increases, a lack of donor retention, and a shrinking pool of prospect names have caused a shift in the way fundraisers use direct mail, but it's a shift, not a post-mortem we're talking about here.

Did you know that...

- If you're trying to find new donors, direct mail is far and away the most successful and cost-effective method.
- Direct mail, not email, is still the method that nonprofits use to ask current donors to give again and to increase their level of giving. We're talking direct mail that is tangible, specific, personalized, and most of all, not boring.

And here's a thought to tuck away until your next appeal: increasingly, we are finding that **direct mail leads to more and more people going online to give than any other channel.**

That's right! **Our clients' results indicate that donors are as much as 3-5x more likely to give an online gift as a result of a direct mail appeal...not an online appeal.**

When you think about it, that makes *direct mail more important than ever.*

To repeat: **today, direct mail works best when the audience is targeted and specific.**

What about your audience? Let's talk specifics:

- *Mailing list* – your list should be updated through NCOA (a permanent change-of-address list through the USPS) and segmented based on location and your relationship to the donor, household, giving patterns, age, and income (to name a few attributes);

- *Your message* – this is your "do or die" moment with your donors and prospects. If your content isn't compelling, it doesn't matter if you do everything else perfectly; your appeal will fail because you haven't taken your audience on an emotional journey. <u>Tell a story about one person, not about your organization's accomplishments.</u>

Many organizations stumble here because they're neither storytellers nor story compilers. If you want to get better at this crucial step in the process, hold training sessions where you teach everyone in your organization –leadership, board members, development staff, program staff, volunteers, maintenance staff, and any other constituency groups I haven't named to be good listeners so they can learn of, and share, stories with others. (see samples in appendix).

- *Printing* – It's very much like a teeter totter. You want to produce a piece that's eye catching, bold and attractive, but that costs money and has to be balanced against the funds you have available. Measuring what's practical against what's most appealing to your donors and prospects means that you should aim for the sweet spot that will strike a delicate balance between what is visually pleasing with what will prompt action while providing enough information that makes it easy for your reader to make a gift.

  Do you really want to incur more costs by including a brochure with your request? I don't think so. We advise against taking away from the reason for sending a letter... the letter itself. The exception to this is an acquisition piece which may very well be going to someone who has never heard of your organization before.

- *Timeline* - Do you know when your donors are most likely to give? For most, it's the holidays, spring, and summer, in that order. For others, the time may be during a significant event or crisis like the coronavirus pandemic. What you need to figure out is the most important time to send your appeal to each of your segments.

- *Follow-up is key* – Are you making sure your donors know how much you appreciate them? You don't just thank donors when you receive a gift. Or do you? There's so much more you can and should be doing. For example, occasional donor-centered newsletters (with success stories of how donations have helped can have a huge impact in your efforts to build long-lasting relationships). Yes, I did say **donor-centered newsletters**. Imagine, for a second, your donors opening your newsletter and being bored to tears by a bunch of statistics as opposed to being caught up in a story about how the Jones family, for example, was able to move out of a shelter and into their very own home. Stories are what donors want to hear about and they shouldn't just be in your appeals.

Are stories more work for you? Probably. But shame on you if you let that stop you because the rewards of using stories in your communications to prove impact far outweigh the work of developing them. Stories bring to life the work you do by using everyday language to create a scene. Here's an example:

For Ginny and her three young children, the past few months have been difficult, to say the least. Ginny had lost her job, been evicted from her apartment, and been alternating staying at her brother's house, motels, and shelters. It was taking a real toll on her family. Her kids' school work was suffering, and everyone was stressed out.

> So, if your organization is making a difference, that's the kind of story you should be telling in your appeals AND your newsletters. Your stories should be showcases to your donors of how they are helping you make a difference for the people/the community you serve.

Things were soon to change though, due to donors like you. *Ginny and her kids are going to be moving into a home of their own.*

That's right--**the high value money is hiding in donor retention**. It's right there for you!

Let's address the "gorilla in the room." While there's nothing like the mail to tell your story, there is a cost involved. We acknowledge that. As far as new donors are concerned, you have to be ready to get a .5 to 1.5 percent response rate, at least in the beginning. In other words, **you'll only be successful when and if you get a new donor to give--and then give again and again.**

The unfortunate part, as already noted, is that very few new donors ever make a second gift to the same organization, while six of ten will make a third gift if you can get them to that point. *(Fundraising Authority)*

One might argue, "Why bother with new donors if it's that difficult getting and keeping them?" Think about it.

During crises, many organizations stop doing donor acquisition campaigns in the name of saving money. By the time the economy improves, pipelines are empty and development professionals are desperate to find new major gift prospects.

That's why consistent, yet wise, donor acquisition is so important. And that's why upper management must understand and view donor acquisition as an investment that will more than pay for itself over time (and not as an expenditure).

But just what exactly am I referring to when I say do donor acquisition "wisely"?

Well, while first gifts are always nice, they're like a first kiss, aren't they? One wonders if it will lead to anything more—like the development of a relationship. It's the second and third kisses, or in our case, gifts, that are more important because, chances are, more commitment is being established. There's a foundation for a loyal and trusting relationship at least beginning to be formed.

Getting that first gift, I'm sure you'll admit, isn't much fun but you don't have to work very hard to get it, do you? The second and third gifts, much like dating, though, that's hard work in the sense that it takes determination to grow relationships—it doesn't just happen overnight.

It's the second gift that determines whether your acquisition efforts bear fruit.

The first mailing that gets you an initial gift is always exciting. But it's the second and third gifts (and so on) that keep a donor giving that's really important.

In that regard, I've had many conversations about the need for new donors, especially in light of fewer individuals making gifts. The need is, after all, greater than ever to "fill the pipeline." Almost always, those conversations include some version of the following: "Our budget is very limited."

That's when I like to suggest that you concentrate your efforts and resources on getting more second and third gifts rather than more and more first-time gifts.

Let me be clear here: is acquisition important? Without a doubt. However, retention and acquisition go hand in hand.

Ultimately, if you gain a new donor, the key is what you do to get that individual to become a loyal donor.

Simply put, your job is to give new donors reasons to continue to be generous.

Here are some things you should be doing to encourage renewed gifts:

- You should be mailing first-time donors a welcome packet <u>within two to three weeks of receiving the first gift.</u>
- You should send them information that both informs and inspires them to give more.
- You should be assuring these donors that they made the right decision when they sent your organization a gift, and that you're deserving of another one.
- You should be educating your new (as well as more established) donors on current happenings via newsletters and updates.
- Above all, you should be telling your new donors what you did, or are doing, with their first gift—remember, donors need/want to see proof that you're putting their money to good use.

At Rescigno's, we've been saddened and frustrated by the number of nonprofits who don't understand the investment involved in doing new donor acquisition. Acquisition is a three-year proposition. So many organizations have poor results after the first year and pull out because the ROI just isn't there. The thing is, it never is after the first year. Repeat after me: *it* takes three years to begin to see a positive ROI on acquisition campaigns.

Here's a valuable lesson from a seasoned development professional and friend, George Boodrookas.

"Everything was going well. Beautifully, in fact. Our annual gala was hitting on all cylinders. The food was great. The entertainment went perfectly. The silent auction was hot... bids on every item, and I was feeling good about my job as the emcee...feeling as one with the audience. Then I turned it over to the auctioneer. You know that feeling when the auctioneer just flat out bombs? Well, I do. Having relinquished my spot on the dais to the auctioneer, I took my seat near the front of the room...and I watched in horror...with a smile glued to my face... sweating large beads of sweat as the evening slipped into embarrassment. It was painful.

This experience taught me a lesson. Don't rely so much on your gala. Diversify your portfolio. Even though revenues from the event were pretty good, I wanted more options in our fundraising strategy. Shortly thereafter, I met Ron and Sue Rescigno at a CASE conference and together we've revitalized our direct mail and messaging to donors, alumni, and friends. Now, even during a healthcare and economic crisis, we're raising more funds than ever for our students and programs. The gala will happen again, if the virus allows, but we won't be so dependent on the outcome...and we're using a different auctioneer."

George Boodrookas, Ed.D.

Dean of Advancement & Executive Director,

Modesto Junior College Foundation

THINGS TO REMEMBER:

- The real money hides in keeping the donors you already have.
- There are two keys to successful direct mail appeals:
    1) A high level of personalization and segmentation.
    2) Stories that shine a light on the problem you and your donors solve on a daily basis.

CHAPTER 4

LESS MAIL = LESS $

Another very important issue to establish is that, simply put, you will raise more money if you communicate with more people.

While speaking on "Donor-centered Appeal Writing" in Norfolk, Virginia, at the Association of Lutheran Development Executives (ALDE) Conference, Sue and I were asked, "Is there a limit as to the number of times you can ask before running the risk of turning your donors off?"

Let me answer the question the way we did then.

I explained that in Oak Lawn, Illinois, where Sue and I reside, during a mayoral election, it's not unusual to get one or two solicitations per day from candidates I have supported in the past. This number of solicitations over a two-month period of campaign time is intrusive and annoying. I don't think many nonprofit organizations would dare, or even have the budget, to mail that often over that length of time. Besides, they add no value to my understanding of who the candidate is, or what he or she stands for or against.

Finally, I summed up my answer to the question by saying that five or six direct solicitations a year sounded about right to me. Now, I know that the usual sequence is a fall, end-of-year, and spring appeal, but in 2019, for the first time in as long as I can remember, we were approached by organizations planning to increase their "three sequence" to four or five. Bully for them!

If giving makes donors feel good, and reporting back to them on the impact of their gifts makes them feel even better, why not give them a couple more opportunities over the course of a year to have those good vibrations?

This may be hard to believe, but I could name many organizations that are asking (via direct mail appeals) 12-18x per year. The point is that **in all the research we've done over our nearly 30 years in business, there is no evidence that contacting donors this often drives them away. Quite the opposite.**

In fact, the less frequently you contact your donors, the less revenue you will have, <u>and you will experience much poorer donor retention in the long run.</u>

Also, the more often you ask donors for gifts, the more likely they are to make them multiple times during that year.

It really is fantastically simple—the less mail you do, the less giving and fewer donors you will receive. Now there's a lesson for you! In fact, one reason many, many new donors never make gift #2 is too few, not too many, communications. You see, donors, especially new ones, have a bad habit. They tend to forget rather quickly whom they gave to.

Warning: more important than mail frequency is mail relevance. If you're speaking to what you know your donors are interested in and giving them many opportunities to "make a difference" in ways that matter to them (and then thanking them in meaningful ways), you can maintain a consistent and high frequency of communications that will be well worth your effort. If, however, you're communicating with your donors in a way that is focused on your organization and the great things it is accomplishing, even just one appeal will be too many.

As to what should be mailed out in addition to the appeals, we recommend:

- Welcome kits for new and renewed donors,
- Three to four newsletters,
- A philanthropy report or annual report,
- Invitations to special "donor-only" events (in addition to online communications).

We've learned that organizations that assume donors will give more, even if they are communicated with less, almost always are disappointed in the end. That's not the way direct mail fundraising works.

The key is communication that is personalized and relevant.

Is it true that donors, especially those who have given over a long period of time, say they don't want to be over-asked by organizations they support? Yes, it is. But if you look at their giving habits, even though they may complain, that doesn't seem to translate to less giving.

Bottom line: if you don't ask often enough and with great

impact, you will leave a lot of money on the table. <u>Have you been leaving money on the table for years?</u>

Helpful hint: with all donors, especially new ones, try sending a questionnaire that asks about how they'd like to be communicated with in the future. Do they want to receive email, annual reports, or annual appeals? How often would they like to receive them? **Our experience is that when asked about their preferred method of communications, donors often stayed with nonprofits longer and at larger average gift size. Simple, right?**

The key behind this strategy of asking donors to choose how they would like to be communicated with is *options or choice*. And it is a great way to build donor trust and loyalty, too.

Allowing donors to choose is often a long-term success marker for nonprofits. Only a relative handful of donors respond by saying, "Take me off your list." Most people never respond, but at least you're giving them a choice.

THINGS TO REMEMBER:

- You can be sure that if you're not asking for a gift via direct mail, your competition is.
- A few communications, including appeals, that are focused on the donors' accomplishments, not the organization's, will resonate with them much more easily than communications that are all about what the organization is doing.

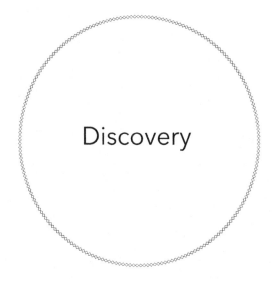

Discovery

CHAPTER 5

—

WHY THE DISCOVERY STEP IS VITAL TO ANNUAL FUND SUCCESS

Now let's go into detail regarding each of the steps in the process beginning with Discovery.

Whether you're a new development director or a seasoned executive director, you very well may not know everything you need to know in order to execute a successful annual fund program.

When we evaluate annual fund programs, we look for challenges or obstacles that may be inhibiting financial growth. More often than not, what we find is that an organization has spent an inordinate amount of time and money on just one step in the annual fund process to the detriment of the others.

It is our external perspective of an annual fund's strengths and weaknesses that allows us to provide unbiased recommendations that, if implemented, will lead to improved revenue.

Here is a list of questions that help us in our first step in **The Process-Driven Annual Fund.**

<u>Annual Fund</u>

What are some of the biggest challenges you are facing with your annual fund?

How many staff members do you have on your annual fund team?

How much did your annual fund make last year?

How much of that came from direct mail response?

Do you have giving societies?

Do you have an annual fund budget for communications?

Direct Mail

How many appeal mailings are you doing per year, and when?

How many are you communicating with for each appeal?

How many segmented groups are you mailing to?

Do your letters ask for a specific amount and do you use personalized ask strings?

What percentage is acquisition (non-donor and long-lapsed donor) vs. renewals?

Data

What database do you currently use? Is it a fundraising software?

Do you currently have a knowledgeable database manager?

How many total records do you have in your database?

What is the breakdown?

> Current Donors (anyone who has made a gift in the last three years)
>
> Lapsed Donors
>
> Non-Donors (those who have never made a gift)

What information do you have on your donors? (Age, education level, net worth, etc.)

Donor Communication

Besides appeals, what other communication do you have with your donors, and with what frequency are they sent?

Welcome kits

Magazines

Newsletters

E-blasts

Annual report

Acknowledgement letters

Holiday cards

Other

The idea behind the Discovery Step is to bring to light weaknesses or obstacles in your current annual fund program. Knowing these issues before you begin the process will help you make informed decisions going forward.

Data, Wealth Screening, Analysis, Donor Profiling

CHAPTER 6

KNOW WHO YOUR DONORS ARE AND WHY THEY GIVE

Now that you understand the importance of direct mail in relation to the annual fund, let's dig deeper into step two of the process of data analysis, wealth screening and donor profiling.

What do you know about your donors, really? The more the better, you know!

Ask any major gift officer and they'll probably tell you that they should pay more attention to annual fund donors.

And, by extension, I'm willing to wager that if you have a planned giving officer, he or she would agree.

Let's consider Mr. or Ms. Classic American Donor may have been giving to you consistently over a number of years but because the gifts don't necessarily fall into the Major Gift category, they've likely gone unnoticed. These donors probably aren't in your plans because they aren't too interested in your events or other aspects of your program. I'm suggesting that you examine your list to find out more about them.

There's money in getting to know more about them. Real money!

What they are is LOYAL to your cause, and, as such, deserve your attention.

Just who are these "typical" donors? There are many ways to differentiate them.

For example, consider age. Over 40 percent of millennials are willing to give via social media, while 43.5 percent of Gen X donors have given via their workplace. Age isn't the only factor that sets donors apart from one another. If we look at donors as a whole, caucasian donors are in the majority compared to the overall proportion of the population.

In fact, the donor universe looks more like the racial and ethnic makeup of America in 1990 than that of today's America. Almost 75 percent of donors today are non-Hispanic whites, even though caucasians make up only 64 percent of the population as of June 2019.

On the other hand, while both African-American and Hispanics are underrepresented in the donor universe, there is no suggestion here that caucasian Americans are "more generous" than other racial groups. African-American and Hispanic donors, in fact, say they are solicited less frequently and would give more if they were asked more often.[1]

To be sure, **fundraising's future lies in the realization that a one-size fits all approach is a thing of the past.**

Therefore, it follows that <u>successful nonprofits are going to need to have a diverse donor base to sustain and grow their organizations' missions.</u>

What about you? Are you creating plans and implementing strategies that will reach all of the people who might be interested in supporting your cause?

Now there's a tip to put into action immediately.

> Tailoring fundraising communications, like the annual fund, to the interests, values, and traditions of African-American, Hispanic, and other ethnic groups, in addition to the approaches traditionally used with white America, is simply common sense as people of color become majorities in communities across America.

In fact, the intelligent use of data is an essential part of fundraising success. Having the necessary insights that determine how to effectively reach out to the right donors at the right time with the right ask amount, is an investment that yields positive results.

One of the first things we do with new clients is to help them create a donor profile. Not simply a wealth screening profile, but a tool to help in donor communications.

These profiles ideally give a detailed description of a particular donor's day-to-day life—their likes and dislikes, philanthropic tendencies, religious affiliation, and political leanings, to name a few.

When you invest the time to do this type of donor profiling, you'll strengthen your development efforts simply by getting to know who your donors really are, and what they're interested in giving to. Ideally, we come up with the "classic" donor—the one who's most loyal and dedicated and most interested in giving to your mission. These then become the donors you want to find more of in your file.

When you do, you should try and imagine the following:

- What other organizations they donate to
- How much they donate to other organizations
- What they do for a living
- Where they live
- How many children they have, if any
- If they go to church and, if so, where

While not a complete list, these are just a few examples of how to understand your "classic" donor and create a donor profile. There are many other ways to understand the people you are appealing to. Think of it like you would if you were dating and you are sincerely interested in knowing more about that other person. Understanding your donor base builds a straight line, transforming your annual fund into a revenue machine.

THINGS TO REMEMBER:

- Do you know as much as you should about your average donors? Your data should provide a profile that can be used in your communications with them.
- Your profile will also guide you in your ask amounts.

[1] www.blackbaud.com

CHAPTER 7

DONORS COME IN ALL SHAPES AND SIZES

Once you know what your average donor looks like, you need to be aware of some basic research regarding donors.

Philanthropic giving from these classic donors happens every day, all across America, from Alaskan villages to New York City. If this falls under the heading of boring, consider this: giving leaves deep imprints on the lives we live because of the depth and intimacy in the way philanthropy is communicated.

Gifts that are the result of moderate support from annual fund donors, accumulate in ways that make all of our lives easier, more interesting, even better.

Among individual donors in the U.S., very many come from average citizens earning modest wages. According to Philanthropy Roundtable's Who Gives, "Six out of ten U.S. households donate to a nonprofit in any given year with their annual gifts totaling between two and three thousand dollars a year."

That's America, and it's what still makes us the country we are. Also according to Philanthropy Roundtable, "Americans voluntarily donate almost 7x as much as Europeans."

When Rescigno's first started working with nonprofit

organizations in 1992, a young donor was defined as being in the 25-40 age range. *Today, a donor is still considered young at 60.*

There is some pretty logical thought inherent in what may seem to be a strange description of a young donor: *donors who are 65 and older make up the majority of American donors.* Those under 35 make up the minority.1

What this should mean to you is that when you're communicating with your donors, in your mind's eye, you should be seeing a baby boomer rather than a millennial (except if the millennial is the segment you're appealing to, of course). When you stop to think about it, the young are almost always going to be the smallest number of givers, if for no other reason than economics. They just don't have the financial wherewithal yet.

People really start to become philanthropic at around 55 years of age. Their kids have finished college, they're making their last payments on their house, and they find they have a little left over at the end of each month. This is when they really start to give to nonprofit organizations. And this giving continues and increases until about the age of 70. It's at about that time that increased giving may slow down, but not stop.

This is especially true <u>if you've been able to develop a strong annual fund.</u> This behavior will usually continue until a life event such as illness or death occurs. In fact, as just hinted at, it probably doesn't come as a surprise that donors in the age range of 80-89 very often have a response rate that is much higher than those aged 30-39.

Is finding out as much as you can about your donors a priority at your organization?

I know of one example where an organization received check #1 from a donor when she was 55. The last gift was received when the lady turned 101—just before she died. Talk about a lifetime of giving! She must have felt very gratified—and that's the point, right?

Rescigno's works with an educational foundation serving a large population. The average donor who supports their mission is 77 years old.

Be aware, however, that making generalizations about age groups is a dangerous game. We do try to use personalization and customized ask amounts, for example, to invigorate personalized communications, but it's really the targeting of clusters of individuals with a message and design that you hope appeals to what you think are common interests, perceptions, desires, and maybe even fears. It's more about playing the percentages and making educated assumptions.

Here are some statistical facts and figures to support many assumptions and generalizations we've come to use regularly:

- Lawyers and doctors are generally very poor prospects for donations. Those marked as "religious," "homemaker," or "retired" were most likely to give.
- Americans with earnings in the top 20 percent of income levels contributed on average, 1.3 percent of their income to charity. Those at the bottom 20 percent donate 3.2 percent of their cash to charity—that's more than double their more-wealthy counterparts.[2]

- People who make between $50,000 and $75,000 give an average of 7.6 percent of their discretionary income to charity, compared to an average of 4.2 percent for those making $100,000 or more.[3]
- "The 'rich' predominantly give to the arts, universities, and sometimes health-care organizations, while the 'poor' tend to lean towards social services and direct-service organizations serving the poor," said Ken Berger, then president and CEO of Charity Navigator in 2012.
- Increasingly, wealthy donors in particular are looking for evidence that their funds are being put to good use. They want to see tangible outcomes.

Knowledge is a grand thing, isn't it?

"But Our Young Donors Are Very Important to Us!"

Maybe you've heard this one before. If you have, indulge me. I once heard a conference attendee ask a speaker what she could do to raise more money from "the young crowd." The speaker's reply was, *"Oh, that's easy. All you have to do is wait until that young person gets older!"*

Maybe your donors are old and dying or just not responding to your messaging. Maybe they're just set in their ways. Maybe you want to concentrate your efforts on Millennials.

Before doing anything drastic, think for a moment. Do you really want younger donors? Of course, you do; you must keep replenishing, right? But consider: an elderly donor base isn't in and of itself a bad thing. It's great news, to be honest.

Older people have more money that's disposable. Add to that the fact that they've learned to give back.

Plain and simple, **older donors are much more valuable. They give more and are more reliable.**

The exception to the above is major disasters or a fad like the Ice Bucket Challenge. That's when we see that younger donors get involved. Outside of that, their giving is rare and their retention is far below that of older donors.

The lesson here is, when donors get older, they'll be in a better position to give and to give more than younger donors. If you've cultivated them properly, that is.

There's really nothing to fret about here. You should be secure in the knowledge that older donors are more loyal and will stick with you longer. They're the better bet.

That's right! Older donors are still "king of the hill, top of the heap, A#1!" That's not changing anytime soon.

Food for thought: maybe you should be targeting those who are on the *threshold of becoming old* (those in their 50s). They'll likely give at roughly the same amount as those in their 60s, even though they'll still have plenty of years of giving still in them. **It makes sense that this would be the group you'd want to be working hard to cultivate.**

Often, we're asked about baby boomers. Think about it: roughly two-thirds of all financial assets in the U.S. belong to them.[4]

Just a few short years ago, there was a great deal of talk about how secure baby boomers were, both in wealth and their willingness to support causes. The belief was "boomers" were going to transform American society.

And then the recession of 2007 happened. As a result, when 2008 rolled around, "boomer" giving had declined by 17 percent. The recession really caused people to take a deep breath and re-consider their philanthropic interests. But it would be inaccurate to say that boomers became stingy. Very inaccurate.

Here's one example of their generosity: though boomers make up about 38 percent of households in America, they're contributions are responsible for just over 50 percent of total charitable contributions.[5]

We expect that boomer capacity to give will continue to increase over time since, in part, almost $27 trillion in inheritances will be passed along in the next 40 years or so.[6]

So, get that shovel out and start digging (I mean researching) for those who will soon be turning old. If you do a good job with boomers, they could (and should) become true heroes to and for your organization.

THINGS TO REMEMBER:

- Donors today are considered young at 60 years old
- The majority of donors are 65+
- Know the demographics of your donors and prospects

1 Target Analytics Group, 2018 April

2 Atlantic Magazine, 2015 June 24

3 The Chronicle, 2018

4 Social Security Bulletin, Vol. 64, No. 4

5 The Next Generation of American Giving, 2019 June 24

6 The Wall St. Journal, 2012, June 11

CHAPTER 8

THE TERRIBLE COST OF NOT DOING ACQUISITION

What if I suggested to you that a place like Dunkin' Donuts spends around $2,000 to acquire a new customer who will start off by spending around $4.00 to $5.00 for a donut and a cup of coffee as they become regular consumers of good old Dunky D? You might say that seems expensive and foolish on their part— until you figured out that the Lifetime Value of this DD customer over the span of 20 years is in the range of $14,000 or so.

How foolish does that sound?

The point is, you have to constantly be growing your donor pool by acquiring new donors. But now, it's easier because you have a profile of your current donors so you know what to look for in potential donors.

Let's get a little more into the deeper ramifications of not having a plan to attract new donors.

Finding new donors is like going hunting. You need to have a good place to hunt and something that attracts new donors, like your mission and impactful programs.

When your organization fails to invest in the acquisition of new donors in order to replace those lost through donor

attrition, and/or to ensure future growth, you're preparing your organization for some very hard times in the future.

Do you think I'm exaggerating or overstating?

You may be doing very well right now. Money may not be an issue because of the support you are receiving annually. Booyah for you!

"Right now" is not the point, however. The future is.

There's not a development director out there, at least that I've ever met, who isn't concerned about finding new donors.

Every year, for a myriad of reasons, many donors stop giving. This being the case, you would think that fundraisers would automatically include a donor acquisition strategy in their overall fundraising plan. However, that's not the case, not even close.

Although it may seem to be a miracle when a donor who is acquired through direct mail makes a gift of significance, you can make it happen for your organization. Here are four "miracles" I learned about in 2020 :

1. A $500,000 endowment was made to an educational organization by a donor acquired through the mail four years previous. Until this endowment, his biggest gift was $500!

2. In November of 2009, during the Great Recession, $200,000 was awarded to a women's shelter from a donor who was acquired through the mail whose largest gift had been $75. A note was attached that simply, but eloquently said, *"I know times are hard; you need this money now."*

3. An organization that helps families of children with illnesses received a $30,000 gift in response to a direct mail appeal. This particular donor had given his first gift of $35 a few years earlier. On the reply card he had crossed out the box that said $25.00 and then wrote in to the "other" section $35,000.

4. An animal welfare organization received a gift of $40,000 from a donor who had previously made gifts only through the mail. The largest gift he had given was $1,500. The donor sent along a note that said, "You don't need to call me, just keep doing a good job for the animals and don't forget to keep sending me letters."

I don't have any verifiable evidence to back this up, but I feel very confident in saying that once these organizations acquire a new donor, what they have in common are the following:

- Warm, personal thank you notes that are sent out in a very prompt fashion;
- Newsletters and other cultivation pieces sent throughout the year that don't ask for money, but carefully explain the difference donors are making in people's lives;
- Staff, volunteers, or board members, who every-once-in-a-while pick up the phone to simply say thank you to donors;
- Direct mail appeals that provide donors with a clear idea of what will be accomplished if they send a gift.

So, for me, what it comes down to is this:

If you and your team are not constantly trying to find new donors (donor acquisition) you're not doing your job. Period.

It's that important. Finding new donors has to be a part of your yearly development plan. Just as losing donors is a natural part of the "gains and losses" that occur in fundraising, so is the need to replace lapsed donors with new ones. And yes, finding the right new donors is important, too, because finding ones that align with your mission is a key ingredient of donors who will support your mission over a long period of time.

If you're not investing in new donor acquisition, here's what will happen sooner rather than later: your file of donors will shrink to the point of drastic decline and, before long, so will your revenue.

With donor acquisition, you get what you are willing to pay for. When you invest in doing donor acquisition properly, you'll be doing the necessary and vital work of securing your organization's future.

Here's how to do acquisition properly:

1. Figure out what your goal is. Look at how many donors you've lost and how many you've gained over the last 5 years. Then pay special attention to specific areas where you've lost the most donors (events, direct mail, major donors, etc.). Based on this knowledge, you should be able to make realistic projections for donor acquisition. Remember, donors need to be acquired in both good and bad times. The Covid-19

pandemic is a great example of acquiring new donors in very bad times. The important thing, though, is that **you shouldn't wait until donors are leaving in droves before trying to find new contributors.**

2. Research has proven that the most cost-effective way of achieving success in donor acquisition is through direct mail, as we discussed earlier. However, you have to be prepared for response rates of .5 - 1.5 percent. Also, if you develop a proper acquisition list, you will be pleasantly surprised when major gift donations come in. A health-care organization that we work with received a $1.8 million gift as a result of a donor acquisition piece. That gift came in year three of their campaign.

Even stopping acquisition for just one year will result in serious shortages of income in the ensuing years. **You must constantly be feeding the funnel of your donor pyramid with new donors.**

I can hear you thinking to yourself this very minute. You're thinking that this kind of a decision is out of your hands. My strong advice is this: *don't let the CFO, CEO, or whomever it is at your nonprofit, make a short-term decision that will* seriously inhibit growth in future years. At the least, don't let him or her cut acquisition of new donors without a fight.

Do you know what your donor retention rate is? And do you know the number of new donors you need to replace those you lose through attrition? Learn these numbers! I wouldn't be a bit surprised if they give you a jolt.

Create a plan that include both acquisition and donor retention. Find creative ways to make it work within your budget.

If you'd like to know the true consequences of cutting your acquisition, consider this: in 2013, The American Cancer Society stopped doing donor acquisition. After the first year, they estimated that they had lost nearly 11 million dollars in revenue. Let that number sink in for a moment! In addition, they unexpectedly saw an immediate impact on donor renewals as well—proof of just how quickly acquisition fills the funnel. They returned to direct mail acquisition the following year.

There was another, much more positive lesson they learned, and that was that for every $1 they spent in acquisition **they made $7 over the next 3 years. In the short term, in other words, you will lose. Long term? You'll gain in a big way.**

Don't just take my work for it; here's what a colleague and friend shared with me about donor acquisition.

"My favorite annual fundraising story happened in the late 1980s. On the surface it seems completely unrelated to fundraising, but it had enormously positive repercussions. I watched a 'motivational business video' (not directly related to fundraising) about 'thinking out of the box.' It was a story of a young man who collected starfish off of a beach, one by one, and threw them back into the ocean. A stranger came by and inquired about the young man's seemingly futile effort of saving the lives of only a few star fish since the sand was covered with them.

Without breaking stride the young man's response was, 'At least I saved this one' as he tossed another starfish into the water.

"Almost immediately, I equated the individual starfish to any unknown donor prospect. I was just beginning the follow-up phase of an annual fund with a database of 60,000 and fairly stable donor base of 15,000. Since I was in a one-person office, my time and efforts at donor segmentation and personal visits were limited. Nonetheless, I kept thinking of these unknown and unreached donor prospects like the starfish 'lying on the beach' waiting to be approached. Heretofore, I had always surpassed my campaign goals and handled all follow-up via direct mail with little personal contact. I stepped out of my comfort zone of juggling a full schedule and began phoning and setting appointments with past (LYBUNT and SYBUNT) donors. I surpassed my annual fund goal that year with the help of an additional 90 major gift and general phase donors representing 9 percent of my $800,000 goal.

"Over the years, the experience helped define my openness to other best practices including the importance of wealth profile searches, comparative data of all campaign phases, direct mail pieces with personalized postscripts, etc. There is a lot to be said for remaining open at any moment to 'thinking out of the box.' "

Joe Langenderfer, CFRE
Executive Director
THE FOUNDATION
of the **Roman Catholic Diocese of Raleigh**

THINGS TO REMEMBER:

- Acquisition must be seen as an investment that will pay for itself, though usually not in the first year.
- Acquisition and retention should be done simultaneously.
- Create plan messaging, segmentation, and timing.

Create a Plan Messaging, Segmentation, Timing

CHAPTER 9

—

A PLAN FOR MORE MONEY

Now that the data has been analyzed and you know who you need to communicate with, let's talk about putting together the plan to raise more money because, almost always, you're expected to raise more money every year, aren't you?

In my former career, I was a high school English teacher for 14 years before becoming a principal. The title of this chapter is a quote from a short story, The Rocking Horse Winner, by D.H. Lawrence. I used to have my classes read this short story back in the 70s and 80s. Today, it perfectly reflects what I hear from nonprofit fundraising professionals who are seeking advice about how to raise 'more money.'

In the story, the protagonist, young Paul, has heard his parents arguing over the need for money. He takes to riding his rocking horse. In the course of doing so, the name of the winner of the local horse race magically comes to him. His parents take that information and bet on the winner. Young Paul's prediction is right, and for a while he helps his parents win more money. But, as time goes on, he finds that he must ride his horse faster and faster in order to "see" who the winner of the next race will be. His parents' need for more money is unrelenting, however, and finally, young Paul rides and rides and rides so furiously that he passes out and dies.

You see, Paul's parents didn't have a plan to earn more money so they just kept pushing him to ride faster, to bring in more, if you will. If they had a plan, it would have eased the burden on young Paul and very probably saved his life.

> Projects will fail without a solid plan, deadlines, consistent follow-up with measurements throughout the entire project, and a clearly understood, shared vision of what success looks like at the end.

Do you have a plan for raising more money? Without one, there can be no vision for growth...for attracting more money to your organization.

Without a plan there is no way for others, especially your board, program staff, volunteers, and donors to understand what they can do to help.

All too often, those who reach out to me are satisfied with not reaching their fundraising goals. Why is that? Is it a lack of accountability or because unrealistic goals having been set for them by the board, for example?

The solution starts when you commit to creating a plan for success. If you're not sure where or how to begin, here are the components of a fairly straightforward annual fund plan:

1. *The goal for the year, based on the organization's needs* and available prospects. In other words, how much will your nonprofit need to raise to perform the activities that meet its mission?

CHAPTER 9: A PLAN FOR MORE MONEY

2. *The case for support* – What do you plan to do with the money you raise?

3. *Tactics*- How will you raise the needed funds? This section gives details. For example, if you need to raise $500,000, some tactics might include:
   - Analyzing your data to make sure you are communicating with the right people.
   - Increasing your prospect pool/acquisition
   - Appeal letters
   - Communication pieces
   - Events
   - Personal visits
   - Retention

4. *The timeline*- Having a timeline forces you to think through decisions and provides important guidance as the year progresses.

5. An accountability chart so everyone knows who is responsible for each step.

THINGS TO REMEMBER:

- Having a plan that you follow will greatly help to reduce anxiety.
- Having a plan creates a structure for continuous improvement.

CHAPTER 10

THE PROCESS-DRIVEN ANNUAL FUND CREATES A PIPELINE OF PROSPECTS

Once upon a time, a policeman spotted a drunk looking for something under a streetlight and asked him what he was looking for.

The drunk says that he has lost his keys. The policeman tries to help the drunk find his keys, but after a few minutes he says, "Are you sure you lost your keys here?"

The drunk says, "No, I lost them in the park."

The policeman then says, "Well, why in the world are you looking for them over here then?"

The drunk says, "Because the light is better here."

When it comes to fundraising and the annual fund, I think it's safe to say that , like the drunk in the scenario I just laid out, the tendency is to look at major gifts and planned giving as the place to find donors who give at exceptional levels. The thing is though, **there can be no major gifts or planned giving without the solid foundation of a thriving annual fund.**

Come along with me on a fanciful journey we've taken with more than a client or two over the years:

Let's say your organization just received a major, major gift. That's right, not just a major gift, but a major, major gift of $10 million. The amount doesn't really matter (ha, ha), as long as you think, major, major.

Your bosses? Oh boy, they're really letting their hair down. Can you say, "Yippee!?" Off in the corner, though, is the annual giving officer, maybe someone very much like you. And he's kind of just shaking his head. You can probably understand and sympathize with him for how he's feeling because he's thinking back to a few years ago when Mr. Major, Major Donor gave his first gift. He checks the database and his guess is correct. The first gift was to the annual fund for $75.00.

And then he remembers the work that began right then and there to nurture the donor with personalized thank you notes and phone calls that were vital in building the relationship. As time went on, the donor gave gifts which escalated from the original $75.00 to $100, $500, $1,000, $5,000, $50,000, $750,000 to $10m.

Major donors don't just appear magically, do they? And they certainly don't fall out of trees like leaves do in the fall. **I'll bet if you checked your database, you'd find that the overwhelming majority of your major donors made their first gift as a result of an annual appeal.**

The point is that most of these "majors" make their initial foray into giving to your organization as a result of being identified and cultivated by you–the annual fund professional.

So, yes, **annual giving is still the #1 indicator** that an individual may give a major or planned gift.

> Annual gifts may never steal the headlines or have a spotlight (like the one our poor drunk had been looking under) shone on them, but they are the strong base of future major giving and of creating a habit of giving.

Annual giving professionals are the ones who do the heavy lifting required for an institution to be able to identify who they should be concentrating their major gift efforts on.

So, when creating your plan, treat your new donors like gold because they are your pipeline for major gift prospects.

A friend of mine, Kate Bousum, Director of Advancement at Child's Voice in Illinois, recently shared this great story with me and believe me when I say this happens more than you can imagine.

In response to a mailed appeal, we had a generous family make a $10,000 gift. This was a past supporter, but never anything significant. It was a surprise and wonderful to receive. We stewarded that family. We sent notes, artwork from those impacted by their gift, made thank you calls, and invited them to special events. They didn't engage a lot, were kind when we talked, but didn't attend events and did not give again for six years. Then in response to a mailed appeal, another $10,000 gift!

THINGS TO REMEMBER:

- There can be no major gifts or planned giving without the solid foundation of a thriving annual fund.
- The majority of major gift donors make their first gift as a result of the annual appeal.

CHAPTER 11

FOLLOWING A DONOR COMMUNICATION PLAN WILL CREATE A HABIT OF GIVING

Perhaps Walt Whitman summed up the importance of creating a habit of giving over 100 years ago when he wrote, *"The habit of giving enhances the desire to give."* That was beautifully expressed.

As I've gotten older, something that those who already are in the habit of giving already know, has become very clear to me:

Giving isn't about meeting the monetary needs of people; it's about investing in their futures.

At Rescigno's, we believe that it takes about three to five years to really create a habit of giving with your donors. Having a written plan allows you to adjust and edit, as necessary.

What is involved? It takes <u>a strong solicitation, acknowledgement, and retention program</u>, and charities such as yours, that really care about building relationships with their donors and are willing to put in the effort pursuing smaller gifts with the expectation that they may lead to larger gifts in the future.

In particular, universities seem to be convinced that this strategy is effective. The stakes are certainly high. For example, many involved in university fundraising believe that getting young alumni to give just a little, $10, or $15, gets donors in the habit. The belief (and hope) is that maybe, years down the road, they'll be able to give a lot.

It's all about creating a pattern of behavior, not just raising small amounts of money.

Here's the "thing" though--from a donor's perspective, it takes more than two or three appeals per year to create the habit of giving, especially if all you're ever doing is asking. You see, habits rely on cues to signal a behavior and the more cues donors and prospects receive in the form of appeals, newsletters, updates, invitations, special reports, etc., the more likely they'll be to form this habit.

Do you have a plan for communicating with your donors with an eye towards cultivating a spirit or habit of giving?

A good donor communication plan includes (in brief):

- Three to six donor-focused appeals per year;
- Genuine, heartfelt, impactful thank you notes or expressions of gratitude;
- Newsletters that are donor-focused several times a year;
- Easy to understand Annual Reports/Impact Reports;
- Welcome packets for new and lapsed donors;
- Special invitations throughout the year;
- Social media daily or weekly.

If you think this stuff doesn't matter, consider the following:

- Half of donors give two-thirds of their annual donations to a single charity.
- On average, nonprofits lose 45 percent of their regular donors per year...many say it's because they felt like the nonprofit didn't really explain to them how important they were.
- Donor attrition between the first and second gift hovers at between 55 and 65 percent.[1] Research agrees that there are special benefits that come from giving, not just receiving. The trick here is to get your donors to understand and buy into this notion—even for their own self-interest. When is giving most likely to become habit forming? When you can convince your supporters what giving will do for them.

Giving or generosity gives back in these ways:

1. Health – studies have shown that generosity reduces blood pressure as much as medicine and exercise. Also, it lowers the risk of dementia, reduces anxiety and depression, and improves pain management.[2]
2. Generosity helps with happiness – Giving of time or money gives the donor an emotional boost. It turns out that feeling good is often the result of doing good. Something happens to us humans as we become adults. Amazingly, at some point we transition from wanting to receive gifts to an understanding that

giving enriches and perpetuates our lives and the lives of others. Many studies have shown that giving money to others will put a bigger smile on our faces than spending money on ourselves.[3]

3. Stress reducer – After hooking people up to heart monitors, researchers found that giving too little in a transaction actually drove up stress, while being generous kept stress down.[4]

Your donor communication plan and messaging should strive to create a habit of giving in your donors. As a bonus, they will be happier and more connected to your mission and give more and more often.

You can get this done by creating communications that are relevant in the minds of your donors; communications that allow them the opportunity to connect the dots between their desire to make a difference in the world and your mission. Always, always, always show your donors that you value their opinions and you will have gone a long way towards creating the loyalty that leads to annual giving.

1 Fundraising Effectiveness Project, 2018 April 12

2 Everyday Health, November 2014

3 Elite Daily, John Haltiwanger, December 2014

4 www.sciencedaily.com/releases/2014

CHAPTER 12

IT'S LETTER TIME/MESSAGING

Once you've analyzed your data and created your plan, the next step in **The Process-Driven Annual Fund** is messaging. In other words, the communications that you send to your prospects and donors.

There are alleged fundraising experts out there who will tell you that a four-page or even a three-page letter will outperform a one pager. One of the reasons we've been pretty adamant about one-page letters as opposed to longer ones is that magical word COST. Adding a second, much less a third or fourth, page does increase cost, no doubt about it.

Here's the other consideration: a poorly written multi-page letter won't do better than a poorly written one to two page letter. This is the case for both acquisition and cultivation. I know that some "experts" say write as much as you need to write to convey your message. Our experience has always been that any appeal that's much more than one page in length loses a reader's attention <u>unless the writing is so over-the-top excellent that the reader can't put it down.</u>

Just remember this: think about what you do (and don't do) when you get home in the evening. If you're like most people, you grab the mail on your way in or very shortly thereafter. You then mosey over to your garbage can and begin to look at that day's mail. By this time, you've begun making piles of what mail you'll keep (like bills) and what you will get rid of immediately. There may be a third pile, and that very well may be where nonprofit appeals land—in the "I'll look at this later" pile.

My point is that most people DO NOT come home after a day's work and put on their robe and slippers and make a cocktail for themselves as they sit down to look at their mail. So, if that's the mental image you have, get rid of it. People today are in a rush to do who knows what.

If you have a writer who writes longer letters, fine and dandy. Let him or her have at it. But make me laugh, make me cry, make me feel something—please!! But please, analyze your mailings and be conscious of your Return on Investment.

Really, the quality of the writing is what matters. Your letter should strive to entertain, grab attention, and keep the reader interested all the way to the P.S.

Great fundraising letters should be easy to read and built for skimming. They should be friendly and have donors at the center of the story as the difference makers they are. They should tell a story that is urgent and specific as to the need that must be met (more on this in a bit).

I've written all kinds of fundraising appeals over the years. I once wrote one for a literacy organization. In it, I explained how the donor's last gift helped a mother learn to read to her child. I felt that was more impactful than saying to the donor that his/her gift helped 230 people learn to read.

And I can remember doing an appeal for a pet organization. The development director wanted to do a story about how the organization had rescued x number of dogs over the past year. I suggested a more heartwarming story of Pluto and how the donor helped the dog find his "home for a lifetime." I felt like that story of Pluto would be more meaningful than mentioning the 550 dogs that had been placed in homes over the past year.

Some simple ideas to remember:

- Know what your donor cares about and write about that.
- Show your donor how he/she can solve a problem.
- Explain why the donor should care about the problem.
- Be clear about what you need ($$$).
- Talk "specifics" –like feeding hungry people, sheltering the homeless, finding a cure for a disease, or scholarships for needy students.
- Give an explanation of what your organization is trying to do to address the problem.
- Your appeal should be urgent and personal (use "you," not us or our or we)
- Tell the donor exactly what you need him/her to do.
- Don't apologize for asking - your cause is a worthy one, right?
- Ask early and late (in the P.S.)
- Be believable. I won't believe you if you tell me my $1,000 gift will end hunger. I will believe you, however, if you tell me it will feed a hungry person for 90 days.

I very recently read appeals from an educational nonprofit organization in the Midwest. The most commonplace "best practices" were ignored almost completely for a long time. Here are a few of their transgressions:

- A three-page letter in which the donor is thanked only once and not until the next to last paragraph.
- A donor letter that doesn't reference their last gift, yet asks the donor to give an unspecified upgraded gift as if he should remember how much he gave to the appeal several months earlier.
- Rather than writing a letter at the sixth to eighth grade reading level, which is what we advise, they chose to write their letter at a college level. I can go on about these letters but you get my point, I'm sure.

On our website, if you don't already have a copy, you can download our Annual Appeal Checklist by going to www.rescignos.com.

And remember to ALWAYS make the donor the hero of your story. Remember, the letter has to be emotional–pull at the heartstrings, if you will. So, by all means, make sure you take the time and space to do that.

"When we're working in nonprofit, and we're really passionate about our mission, we forget how people perceive our mission out there in the greater community. Donors want to give back or to be empowered or do something, and we tend to tell our story with a focus on us instead of the focus on what donors need and want from an organization." (Barbara Cohen, Executive Director at Animal Cancer Foundation)

THINGS TO REMEMBER:

- The stories you tell in your appeals should be about how donors can help solve problems.

- The donors are the heroes, not the organization.

CHAPTER 13

INSPIRE X3 AND EDUCATE X1

Let me stay on the idea of writing the appeal for a bit. When you write your appeal, you should try to visualize the common man and woman because that's who the recipients of your direct mail appeals are more often than not.

Remember this: one of the goals when you compose your letter is to help your reader's brain work its way through your letter as easily as possible.

Imagine going out for a walk on a cool fall day. That's what you should be thinking about doing with the appeals you write. Make the experience fast and easy to read as well as emotional—but not too teachy or preachy.

At Rescigno's, we make it a point to work with our clients to make sure that the story they tell is within the "reader comfort" spectrum. And again, we do have a checklist for that!

Occasionally, one of our clients will push back against this suggestion:

"We're the School of Bombastic Verbosity. Many of our best donors are very highly educated. It would be counter-productive and maybe even insulting to them, if we didn't talk to them at their level."

To which I usually respond, "Oh, poppycock!" I don't really say "poppycock," but there have been times I've wanted to.

My point is, though, **that appeal-letter writing is not about impressing your readers; it's not about communicating with them at their level. It is about communicating as clearly and emotionally as you possibly can, the opportunity they have to make a difference in the life of another person.**

It's not as easy as writing an organization-centered appeal, which is all about your accomplishments. Those kinds of letters don't make donors feel anything.

<u>But believe me when I say writing a letter where you make the donor the focal point of the story and where you clearly spell out his or her impact on the beneficiary is what brings in the best results.</u>

And I can't talk about writing personalized appeals without also talking about **segmenting your appeals** to make them just that—personalized!

You should know who the various audiences are that inhabit your database. You should also have an understanding of how they feel about your cause.

Segmenting your donors, and interacting with them based on certain behaviors they exhibit, will lead to better results. When you understand and speak to specific donor likes and dislikes (some would say preferences) the result will be more donor retention and loyalty. Why? Because they'll feel like you know them for more than the check they may send or the gift they make online.

Here are some of my suggestions for segmentation that work really well:

- Change just a couple of lines in your appeal to show that you recognize that the individual is a current or loyal donor. Likewise, do the same to recognize LYBUNTs, SYBUNTS, and long lapsed donors.
- Address MAJOR DONORS personally. If that means personally signing letters to them rather than digital signatures, do it. You'll be glad you did.

For example, *"We depend on loyal, committed friends like you who help us ease the burden of others. Please, if you can, send your gift today. And thank you so very much!"*

- Change a paragraph or two for LEADERSHIP CIRCLE or GIVING SOCIETY MEMBERS. Recognize the donor's level of support and thank them for their leadership.
- Address GROUPS like board members, staff, volunteers, new parents, patients, and alumni in ways they will recognize and identify with.
- For example, "Because you have trusted in Emerson to give your youngster the experiences that will challenge him to achieve greatness, you are a real hero to and for us."
- A letter with a specific message, testimonial, and story about a SPECIFIC AREA OF SERVICE may serve well in inspiring your donors to give generously, especially if they've had a personal experience in that area.

For example, *"At Long Meadows Rehabilitation, no one is more important than you, the patient. We hope that during your recent time with us we exceeded your expectations."*

But don't let segmentation of your appeal intimidate you. Try a few variations for segments that you think will have impact, then stay consistent with what works. When all is said and done, segmenting is one of the best things you can do to build relationships with your donors.

Your appeal should read like a personal letter from the signer of the letter to the recipient. It should be conversational.

Think of it as you and a trusted friend sitting on a park bench having a heart to heart. When we talk with our nonprofit clients and they tell us they're coming up empty on ideas for their next story, I like to suggest that they think departmentally. Who have they had recent conversations with? Was it the head of maintenance, the dean of the school of engineering, or the social worker who just helped place a homeless person? My point is, the stories are to be found in the trenches. If you want a good one, go to the sources that have the experiences in the field.

I read something once by noted fundraising specialist Tom Ahern. He said, "We (meaning fundraisers) write letters at 1 mph. Readers though, read at 100 mph. Things that are said just once tend to be overlooked. When you read direct mail at 1 mph, it can sound choppy. That choppiness disappears at 100 mph."

I don't know about you, but that quote makes a lot of sense to me.

THINGS TO REMEMBER:

- The appeals you write should be written to inspire the "common man" to give. Picture him or her, not a genius, when you write.
- Don't try to impress, try to relate.

CHAPTER 14

RAISING AWARENESS VS. RAISING MONEY

What we assume without really knowing can get us in trouble, can't it? Boards and some leaders love the idea of "awareness raising" because it doesn't involve fundraising or because the belief is that it will lead to more dollars without actually having to ask. In other words, *"Until we raise more awareness about who we are and what we do, we can't be expected to raise much money."*

Wrong! Losing at raising money is what that is. If this is the direction you're going, slam on the brakes. If I were face-to-face with you right now, I would say, *"Are you serious?!"*

Personally, when I think of *raising awareness campaigns,* no image or feeling comes to mind. It's too non-specific. There is no urgency.

> When you try to raise money for things that donors can't wrap their hands, hearts, or minds around, you're going to be disappointed with the results. I promise you will.

Days, weeks, and months often go by without a clear definition of what "awareness" means, or what expected outcomes (like financial support for research) are expected to come from it. Good idea, but a lost opportunity in terms of fundraising.

Which brings me to ask a simple question. **What is your most pressing need? I'll answer for you—money, right? It should be thought of at your organization as the air you need if you're going to breathe. And it's your donors who provide that air in the form of their financial support, not those you serve—not children, sick people, students, the homeless, or the environment.**

Why not? Because if you don't have financial support, you won't be able to help anyone.

Money. You never have enough of it, if I'm not mistaken. Am I wrong about that?

If someone's been whispering in your ear that before you ask for money the public's awareness has to be raised, you're being bamboozled. If that's how you're operating, you're wasting time and money while getting no support in return.

To me, an awareness campaign on limited resources is like drinking Dom Perignon when you only have enough in your budget for a Schlitz or a Pabst Blue Ribbon. I guess I'm showing my age, but I think you get the picture. Personally, I don't partake, but I know enough to know that it's wasteful and irresponsible.

Over the years, what I've learned is that you don't

necessarily have to be familiar with a nonprofit to respond to an ask. First, last, and always, <u>nonprofits should be raising money— yes, **before** wasting money on an awareness campaign.</u>

There's one exception to this. Some years ago, we worked with a community college, and still do as a matter of fact. They had never reached out to their alumni. We suggested including a specific group of alumni in their newsletter mailing that was coming from the college's marketing department before any solicitations were sent. We believe it's important to include all your donors and prospects in your marketing communications.

When you fundraise, what are you doing? You're telling people about who you are, what you do, and why you do it and, hopefully, creating for them a path that allows them to see how they can make a difference through their support of your work. If you do this well enough, they give you money. And guess what you're also doing when you take this approach? You're raising awareness.

THINGS TO REMEMBER:

- In most cases, it's much more important that you are involved in raising money rather than simply awareness before you ask.
- Financial support is the air your organization needs to breathe.
- If you communicate your message effectively, you will raise both awareness and financial support.

Chapter 15

GRAPHICS MATTER

Instinctively, you understand that an image of a happy kid might project or give the impression that the need for support is not great. The kid is happy—what's the problem? Those trusted instincts also are implying that sad kids depress a donor rather than lifting his or her spirits. And goodness knows, you don't want a depressed donor on your hands.

So, what's a development professional to do?

Some things about matching images and photos that are time-tested truths:

1. If your words say "people are starving and desperately need your help," but your photos show happy, well-fed people, your overall message is going to be skewed. Make sure your photos don't contradict your message.

2. Readers of your appeals focus on people, even if your topic is a thing like machines or equipment, have a person (or an animal if it's an animal welfare organization), in the photo.

3. Photos where eye contact is being made are more compelling than photos with little or no eye contact.

4. No frowns or looks of disdain. These send clear, negative messages.

5. Don't use photos that are posed or stock photos. Instead, go for candid shots. Those are much more interesting.

6. Use captions to convey your central message. We believe that photos with captions get read more than anything else in an appeal letter.

If you're a children's organization, a photo of a sad child is likely to raise about 50 percent more than a photo of a happy child. I believe that if pictures of kids are not shown, donors will never embrace the need and therefore fail to see them as really existing.

There are those who believe that negative emotions link to survival instincts and therefore convey an urgent need which compels giving. Still others will say that a positive image is reassuring to donors and indicates that your organization is involved in making good things happen.

Digging Deeper into This

Let's think for a moment about who you're appealing to. While the majority of your donors may, in fact, be what I call "ordinary, everyday" donors, there are other categories of donors in your file, as well. For example, donors who give at a certain threshold that surpasses that of "ordinary" gifts.

Let's take a closer look at your major donors' motivations for giving and how they affect behavior.

This is really important because these donors are giving

you their support at a significant level above and beyond that of "ordinary" donors. This level of donor is interested more in results than in what you do or how you did it.

In the case of major donors, rational appeals (as opposed to emotional ones) are at the root of successful requests for funds.

To be more specific, a donor might be defined as an individual that provides low-level, often sporadic financial support that's not necessarily connected to the mission of the nonprofit.

On the other hand, a major donor is one who usually makes a larger financial commitment that runs over a number of years. **This level of donor is concerned with the long-term success of your organization.**

If we could read the mind of a major donor to your organization, he/she might be saying, *"If you can't show me the results (outcomes), then don't ask me to support your work. And if the results aren't meaningful to me, I'm not interested in helping you."*

Major donors, therefore, might be defined as being interested in changing the lives of your beneficiaries and making real change happen over the long haul. What they need from you is communication which is clear and not necessarily emotional as much as rational, despite the research that donors respond more to emotions than they do to statistics. **For your high-end donors, prove your worth, don't "just" tell a story filled with emotion.**

> They want to see a return on the investment that they've made. They may turn away, rather quickly, from emotional appeals that don't show specific impact.

So be sure to adjust your appeal content and imagery according to the goals and motivations of your various audiences.

At this point I want to be sure that there is a clear understanding of the distinction I'm making between annual fund vs. major gift donors and while this may seem contradictory to advice we've already given, really, it's not. You must take into consideration the audience you are appealing to and what they are most likely to respond to.

THINGS TO REMEMBER:

- The photos you use should convey the tone you have set in your letter.
- Consider your audience when writing the letter and choosing your images.
- Direct Mail donors require a different strategy than major gift donors

CHAPTER 16

MYTH: TEACH DONORS TO UNDERSTAND YOUR WORK AND THEY'LL GIVE MORE DOLLARS, MORE OFTEN

Uh, no! At least, not today. <u>Organizations that adopt an approach that constantly preaches at donors about what they think the donor needs to know, or about what they want the donor to know, run a serious risk of alienating them.</u> We've seen this with any number of organizations we've worked with, both big and small.

Their belief can best be summed up this way: *"When we get a new donor, they come to us not knowing much about the work we do. We need to educate them so they respect us and our work. If they understand what we do, they'll give us more."*

While this may seem contradictory to what was discussed in an earlier chapter, really, it's not. Remember, for major donors, we're talking about emphasizing "results" or "outcomes," not spending time on what you do or how you do it.

The reality is that if your organization could say some

magic words that would alleviate world hunger, for example, your donors would be extremely proud to support you. They wouldn't need to know too many details because what most donors care about is if their gifts of support help in solving a problem they'd like to help solve. Now that's what I mean when I say add "value" to your communications.

Do you have a program that works? Can I be part of the solution? That's enough for most donors. How you solve it isn't nearly as important as being able to tell donors "why" you are engaged in the business of finding a solution that works. They don't need to know the name of the program or any associated data.

I'm reminded of a story I heard:

A major donor prospect was being given a tour of a hospital by the executive director when they came upon a janitor in an elevator. The executive director and the janitor both had worked at the hospital for some time and often said hello to each other as they passed in the halls.

After exchanging pleasantries, the donor asked the janitor how long he had worked at the hospital and what his responsibilities were. The janitor's reply surprised and delighted both the executive director and the prospect. The janitor said, "I help to heal people by making sure this hospital is spic and span. That's why I take pride in keeping this place as clean as possible." In simple, succinct words the janitor perfectly summed up not the "what" of his work at the hospital, but "why" he did what he did.

That's what donors want to know about; not what you do, but **why you do it. Do well sharing this passion for the cause and you will succeed in the annual fund and fundraising in general.**

Can your people do the same?

Your organization's impact on people is what's important. Not your organization. Those may seem like harsh words, but I really believe them to be true. The impact, the difference you're making is what counts most of all. Your organization is the vehicle or conduit bridging the gap between the donor on the one end and the beneficiary of the donor's generosity on the other.

So, instead of trying to educate donors about the work your organization does, take them on a virtual reality trip in which you share with them how they are the real heroes and the ones who make a difference; not the organization, but the donors who support the work of the organization.

Here are some suggestions that have proven successful when it comes to making donors feel special:

- Explain to your donors that they have the opportunity to help solve a problem; Explain what will happen if the problem is not solved;

- As often as you can, make it about the donor *("you made this possible"* or *"you can make this happen"),* instead of about the work you do *("we fed 200 people last Thanksgiving");*

- Address your donors, your heroes, really, by name—so they will feel more connected to your organization;

- Make the connection between the amount the donor gave and the need that it met. Example: *Your $25 gift means that three young children will start the school year with new backpacks.*
- Provide your donors with metrics that are positive and back up your claims of success. Remember to highlight what the donor has accomplished;

These suggestions are just a few of many. They are limited only by your creativity.

THINGS TO REMEMBER:

- You should be able to explain to your donors "why" your work is important, not just what the work is that you do.
- Be clear when explaining to donors and prospects how they can be a part of the solution to a problem.

CHAPTER 17

THE DONOR DID IT - NOT YOU, SILLY... THE DONOR!

Remember the heavy flak President Obama got when he said of small business owners, "If you've got a business, you didn't build that, somebody else did." Whether wittingly or not, dear old Barack, in one clumsily structured sentence, demeaned the working-class entrepreneurs of America. Cut them to their core. That belongs to history now. However, his words remain a great lesson in the type of thing not to say to donors - either directly or indirectly.

<u>Always, always, always give your donors, not your organization, the credit for the difference they are making</u> in the lives of those your mission serves.

When we talk with development professionals about creating **a culture of philanthropy** within their organizations, we emphasize **putting the donor at the center of everything the nonprofit does.**

Whether it's an appeal letter, a newsletter, on the website, or in other communications, making donors the focal point of all you do is a very smart move.

Unfortunately, some very well-known organizations

go about this in the wrong way. They assume that it's more important to explain how fantastic their programs are before asking for a gift.

Yes, educating donors as to the great work done at your organization is important. But in an appeal or as an overall strategy, it's self-serving and, frankly, uninspiring.

More importantly, **if you can shift the focus from talking about the work you do to why and how donors are making a difference in the lives of your beneficiaries, you will benefit greatly. Guaranteed!**

As an example of this, we once worked with a children's organization in the Midwest and helped them change a few things about their appeal, which customarily was mailed three times a year to about 25,000 individuals. The results had been poor for a number of years.

We convinced them to try something a little different. Where they were touting their world-class services, we suggested thanking donors and providing them with impactful stories. Instead of an organization-focused appeal, we helped them send a warm and personalized letter with the word "you" appearing as often as possible. The result was that giving increased 30 percent the first year.

THINGS TO REMEMBER:

- Always make the donor the hero of your organization. Be clear that without their help your nonprofit would be much less impactful.

- What your organization does isn't nearly as important as showing donors and prospects how they can make a real difference in people's, or even one person's life.

CHAPTER 18

WHOSE NECK IS IT ANYWAY?

Over the years, we've helped over seven hundred nonprofits with the execution of their annual appeals.

Inevitably, I've gotten smack dab in the middle of some good old-fashioned spats between development directors and board members and/or executive directors who want control of what goes into an appeal. Now, mind you, they don't want to do the leg work that it takes to write the appeal; they just want final say so over the content.

It's the number one complaint I hear from development directors I'm working with on letter content.

My best advice to nonprofits is that **this should be the responsibility of the development director (unless you have an annual appeal director or someone similar)** until and unless he/she proves this isn't a strength. Only one person should have final approval and that's the person who is going to be judged by the appeal's results—and that's usually the development director.

I think this is only fair. Second-guessing from a board or boss untrained in the art and science of donor communication should be considered a technical foul punishable by, well, I'll leave that up to you.

Some common complaints:

- *"My boss loves to write, but he's so boring."*
- *"My executive director won't let me use a P.S. in our appeal. He thinks it's undignified."*
- *"My boss says our donors are unique, so normal rules don't apply."*
- *"The diocese thinks spending money on appeals is wasteful because no one reads them anymore."*
- *"The chair of our board doesn't like letters that come right out and ask for a specific gift amount so we're not allowed to do that."*

If you're a board member or a boss and you're reading this, you should feel free to make suggestions. But, please, when you undermine your fundraiser's confidence as you demand that the appeal be done your way, in effect, what you're saying is, "I don't have enough confidence in you. I don't trust that you have the knowledge necessary to bring in the money."

If this is you, and you're wondering why you can't keep a development director or an annual fund director around for more than a year or two, perhaps we've just stumbled across an explanation. What do you think?

One more thought on this. If you're the boss, and the appeal your development director wants to send out makes you apprehensive because it's too focused on soliciting, **you may have a winning appeal on your hands. Also, if you and the chair of your board both think the ask is too "in the face" of your donors, then you can be pretty sure that it will work well.**

The lesson here is that <u>leaders must hire talent they believe in and then have enough respect for them to let them do their job.</u> In other words, oversee, by all means, but get out of the way!

Here are some of the qualities I perceive in effective fundraising leaders:

- Passion, not just interest—for the mission and for donors
- A great work ethic and lots of energy
- A people person rather than an introvert
- A person who digs for the facts
- A person who understands fundraising basics and practices them instead of going for the quick fix
- A person that knows his personnel's strengths and weaknesses
- A person who is comfortable letting others take credit for accomplishments

THINGS TO REMEMBER:

- The annual fund is your baby, embrace it and be the expert your organization needs you to be.
- Always fight for the fundamentals of fundraising and educate your leaders.
- Work for an Executive Director who appreciates and understand fundraising.

CHAPTER 19

WHAT'S YOUR STORY?

Sue and I have been urging organizations to tell their "story" for some time now. It's crucial to their and your success as professional fundraisers. My opening question to YMCA development officers at their conference in San Diego was the title of this chapter. We were making a presentation on creating a cultural of philanthropy and wanted to stress the point that one of the main ways of doing this is by making sure everyone understands the organization's story.

Lots of development professionals seem to have trouble with this. I can't emphasize enough how very important the story is in writing your appeal letters.

When I ask someone to tell me their story, they usually start by describing what their organization does.

Don't do that!!

Start by explaining **the why**. In other words, **if you're a food depository that gathers food to distribute to various pantries—that's what you do. But why do you do it? That's your story.**

So, what is your story? "We help keep people of all ages from suffering from hunger."   That's a great example of why an organization does what it does. It has the makings of a great story.

If I were to ask you right now to tell me yours, could you? Not what you do, but **why you do what you do**. As a fundraiser, I'm sure you're a talented, hardworking person. Why have you chosen to be a fundraiser instead of looking for a higher paying job in a different profession? That's the kind of story to tell.

What are your difference-making stories? Have you talked to those who have benefitted from your work (your beneficiaries) lately? Believe me, they have stories to tell.

- If you're in healthcare, you might seek out someone in research who can help connect donor dollars to a new breakthrough medical treatment.

- If you're in education, look for the teacher who is doing innovative work in his classroom with his students. What is he doing? "Oh, he does innovative work." That's great, but explain why he is doing it. For example, he's done X,Y,Z, in his classroom because he is passionate about something. When you explain the motivation, you're explaining the **why**.

Recently, I was asked by a healthcare organization what was trending in storytelling. I suggested to them that they think a little outside the box and tell a story from a different perspective. Instead of telling the story of a patient whose life had been saved, they told the story from the point of view of a pacemaker that saved a man's life. The pacemaker went on to describe all the good that the person was doing as a result of having been given a new lease on life.

THINGS TO REMEMBER:

- Why does your organization exist? If you can answer this question adequately, you will earn more money.

- Take the time to gather and share stories with your staff, board members, volunteers, program directors, etc., and you will find amazing stories to share with your donors. And, as an added bonus, you will go a long way towards helping to strengthen the culture of philanthropy at your organization.

CHAPTER 20

STORIES CAN BE SUPPORTED BY STATISTICS

I read recently about studies that have shown that stories about people cause a chemical to be released by the brain resulting in more individuals being willing to be of help to others; for example, donating money to an organization affiliated with the story.

The drivers that cause neurochemicals to be released in our brains are fairly well known. There's dopamine, serotonin, and oxytocin. Quite a trifecta of giving. Anything that an individual does that increases the production of these "Big Three" causes a boost in mood. More happiness=more passion for your cause!

But that's not all. Serotonin, for example, helps with better sleep, digestion, memory, and appetite. Dopamine is connected to motivation and arousal, and oxytocin has a powerful effect on both the brain and body. Get that oxytocin pumping and even your blood pressure improves. An added bonus is that bonding increases, as well. You do want to build a closer bond with your donors, right? Oh yes, trust and empathy are also enhanced.[1]

If the act of giving lets the human body secrete these chemicals all at once, maybe we should be talking about it to our donors. I'm only half kidding. Which leads to this: when you read statistics, does the information make you think happy thoughts or have happy feelings? Almost all of the time the answer will be a resounding no.

Therefore, **when it comes to statistics or stories, choose stories that make people "feel" some emotion.**

Here's an example:

The first time Jerome took a shower in his new bathroom, he cried. That's because it was the first time the 85-year old had a bathroom to shower in.

"We were poor my whole life and a bathroom with hot and cold running water was something I just couldn't afford. If I think about it, I'll cry some more." (Jerome)

Jerome loves the staff of Northern Living Improvements who transformed one of his rooms into a bathroom. For him, outhouses are now a thing of the past.

This project is part of the nonprofit's focus on repairs and renovations that can help people stay in their homes as they age.

Even though Jerome had a job as a street sweeper, he had been unable to afford a bathroom for his family which included his wife and six children.

One day, one of Jerome's daughters was speaking to a representative of senior services who asked what Jerome could use. She said a bathroom.

I hope from the above abbreviated example you can see the makings of a story that uses emotion as a primary motivator of action.

To be clear, you want action, not thought from your donors. Trying to cause people to act by being rational is knocking on the wrong door. Emotion is what leads to action.

> Fundraising and the annual fund will always be about your ability to touch your reader's emotions as you inspire them to give. So when you're talking with your various audiences, if you need a story to tell, tell about your shared accomplishments with your donors. Refer to things you're proud of, but also be sure to discuss challenges. Donors, especially those donors who are considering making a major gift, don't simply give to solve problems. They also give because they want to be a part of a team that is successful.

Unfortunately, in Chicago, there is a perfect example of this. We are constantly bombarded on radio, television, and news outlets with the number of deaths in the city on any given weekend. The sheer volume of shootings that lead to young people (mostly) being killed is staggering. We become immune to it because the numbers are so large.

Famously, President Trump made these numbers (nearly

800 killed in 2016) national news by threatening to "call in The Feds." Yet, until the summer of 2020, there had been no national outcry. The reported number of deaths represented by these statistics fails to inspire emotion or feeling, wouldn't you agree? And they haven't motivated anyone to act. And that's why, when you communicate with your donors in all of your multi-faceted ways, you should, at all cost, not make statistics the focal point of your messages.

Instead, commit to stories that stir emotions.

And here's a new wrinkle to storytelling that I've never talked about before.

New studies (microedge.com) show that using facts and data to support the story you're telling actually add context and perspective to them. I've underlined "to support" to emphasize that data and facts should support the story, not be its focal point.

Think about it–people want to know whether their support of your mission was impactful. That's exactly why the dollars invested in a nonprofit should tell the story of the impact of those dollars on participants, communities and the issues that are being supported.

What I'm suggesting here is to use supporting data to prove, not illustrate, your impact. Increasingly, what people want to know is specific impact. In other words, explain to your donors how their support resulted in a change of behavior, health benefits, or a marked decrease in violence in a particular community, etc.

Here's an example of one such story that's about a person with facts and figures merely serving as "supportive" information:

In 1987, little Baby J was just 18 months old. She had wandered into her family's backyard and fell into an open well. The well was only eight inches in diameter but that was all it took for Baby J to fall in. She was lodged 22 feet underground.

Within three minutes of arriving, police and rescuers determined that the well was too narrow to try and dig straight down to rescue her. Instead, rescuers planned to drill a hole parallel to the well and tunnel sideways to the spot where the baby was trapped. They devised a contraption, but the jackhammers they had planned to use weren't effective in digging next to a person.

It took nearly 58 hours to finally get to Baby J and rescue her. What happened next is the really remark- able thing about this story: President Ronald Reagan said that everyone in America had become Baby J's godmother and godfather. There was a made-for-TV movie about her, and she and her parents appeared on Live with Regis and Kathy Lee. A photo of her rescue went on to win a Pulitzer Prize.

Amazingly, Baby J, the young girl who was safely rescued after 58 hours trapped in a well, amassed over $800,000 in donations – an impressive amount of money for back in 1987.

What if I told you that, unlike Baby J, there are over 66 million girls in other countries who don't have access to a good education? What if I also told you that these girls, without access to education, are more likely to be sexually abused than they are to attend high school?

Would this mean that we could expect that if we were to broadcast this figure of 66 million girls on CNN for 58 straight hours that those girls might each receive $800,000 as did Baby J?

Of course not. So **why does the one story of just one girl who was trapped in a well for 58 straight hours generate so much response, while, at the same time, a story of so many more girls does not generate anywhere near the same response?**

Some have called it the Easily Identified Victim theory. The victim is a cause for an outpouring of support. Yet, when the need is enormous (66 million girls) the response is negligible.

In one famous survey, researchers walked up to university students and asked them if they'd be willing to answer a brief survey in exchange for $5.00. The survey asked questions about a particular product, but the survey itself didn't matter because the researchers were more interested in what happened when the students received their $5.00.

When the survey was completed, each student was given five one-dollar bills along with an envelope and a letter.

They were told that they had an opportunity to donate any portion of their earnings to the Save the Children charity and were asked to read an enclosed letter. Half of the letters shared information about a statistical victim-so imagine facts and figures from the website of Save the Children. The other half received a picture of a real girl and information about her, also taken from the charity's website.

Participants who were told about one real person donated over twice as much as those who were told about the much larger problem, but in the form of statistics.

In the end, simply sharing one specific person generated much more action than that of the much larger statistical problem.

> *"If I look at the mass, I will never act. If I look at the one, I will."*
> (Mother Teresa)

For nonprofits needing to raise money, this has huge storytelling implications. The evidence in support of the idea that a single story will raise more awareness and money than a statistic is overwhelming.

Sort of like a before and after picture—only more authentic.

Clearly, stories have the power to inspire people to make important decisions about creating positive change.

> Think about your story this way. Who is the villain? Is it a disease, injustice, abuse, or some other terrible blight on society? Now, paint a picture of the victory achieved because of the heroic actions of your donors (with your organization being the vehicle through which the victory happened).

Organizations that are experiencing the best results are packaging their stories **with just enough data** to convince people to help their missions.

<u>Remember to connect your story of one individual to the story of how people have benefitted—the before and the after—the hero's conquest of the villain!</u>

THINGS TO REMEMBER:

- If you want action, use statistics to offer a more complete understanding of the emotional story you tell.
- Help your reader imagine what things are currently like and what they will be like if a gift of support is given.

1 Psychology Today: The Neuroscience of Giving, 2014 April 24

HERE'S A LITTLE "FUNNY" FOR YOU:

Because our development office raises funds for a congregation of religious women, on nearly all of the response envelopes we send to our donors we include a place for them to write their prayer intentions. As you can imagine, our Sisters take the job of prayer for our benefactors very seriously.

The prayer requests can be quite interesting. One elderly donor is very faithful in sending donations and also in sending very specific prayer requests, including that we pray for her cat's kidneys and that she "win a lottery of at least $1,000."

These requests always make us chuckle, but we understand these requests are very important to her. With a bit of careful rewording, we add this benefactor's prayer requests to the list we send to our sisters.

Katherine Barth
Development Director
Sisters of the Holy Family of Nazareth
310 N. River Road, Des Plaines, IL 60016-1211

Acknowledgement Program

CHAPTER 21

DONORS GIVE TO YOU... AND OTHERS

You have sent your appeal out and you're receiving lots and lots of gifts! Now what? It's vitally important to act quickly because, on average, we estimate that the nonprofits we work with share their "everyday donor" with about five other organizations during the course of a given year. That's right, your average donor doesn't just belong to you and you alone. The nerve!

Here's the scary part. **Each and every year charities come snooping around for new gifts–from your donors, both loyal donors and those who are first timers. And if they present a more compelling case for support--need I say more?**

The question becomes, what's a nonprofit organization like yours supposed to do to thwart these interlopers from completely stealing your donors?

Right off the bat, there are two things you can do immediately:

1. *Thank better*--by getting your acknowledgement letter out in 48-72 hours, and make personal phone calls to the donors.

Sue is fond of telling the story of a lady who volunteered at a hospital in the southwest suburbs of Chicago many years ago. One day she received an appeal letter from the hospital. They had not included her in their communications for over 20 years, but did so this time in an attempt to find "lost friends." The lady, now living in Arizona and well into her 80s, was surprised and delighted to hear from the hospital. She loved the story. She was at a place in her life where she was now able to make a gift to the hospital. She sent a check for $250.

Sue had been after the VP of this hospital to make more calls to new donors. Finally, he called her. After thanking the lady and exchanging pleasantries, the VP said goodbye. He said he felt good about the call. The story doesn't end there though. From that point forward, whenever the lady received an appeal from the hospital, she would send another $250. Naturally, the VP would follow up with another call of gratitude. These two people, the VP and the wonderful old lady, began to get to know one another a little bit. During one of their conversations, she had shared with the VP that no one from the hospital had contacted her in many years. One day, the VP received a letter from the lady's lawyer. She had passed away and left the hospital a gift of $1.8 million. True story.

2. *Report more often and more meaningfully* - The process of thanking donors and reporting back to them is a one-two punch for setting up your next ask.

If you don't have an acknowledgement (thank you) program in place, you need one.

Here's the truth about why perfecting your organizations thank-you strategy makes sense. As I've already mentioned, almost two-thirds of first-time donors don't make a second gift. The reasons are really simple—**the thank you you're sending out isn't prompt or meaningful enough.** That's a devastating one-two punch in the wrong direction, if you ask me.

I'm not too proud to say that in my youth I never understood the point of thank you letters. My mom would insist, "You've got to send a thank-you letter." A week or two after my birthday my mom would ask, "Have you sent Aunt Josie a thank-you letter yet?" "Mom, don't worry about it, I will." And then after another couple of weeks had gone by my mom would ask again. Before the word "no" was even out of my mouth my mother would say to me, "If you haven't sent that letter by this afternoon, you're grounded." "Mom, can't I just thank Aunt Josie the next time I see her?" I'd end up doing it, but under protest. I felt like there was no point. My aunt knew I was appreciative.

Thankfully, I wised up as I got older and understood that timeliness and real gratitude were important factors in continuing to get gifts from family members. I figured out that writing really sincere and funny thank-you letters to my relatives was really important to them. I'd be over at their house and suddenly see my thank you on their refrigerator door. Sometimes it would be left up there for weeks or months at a time.

One year, when our son, Dominic, was in college, he didn't have enough money to purchase gifts for Christmas for extended family members. He decided to write letters expressing how important they were in his life. In other words, truly heartfelt sentiments. To this day, these family members still talk about how much those letters meant to them.

How do you treat your donors after receiving a gift? Do you wait four weeks or more to send a thank you, or just not send one at all? You may be saying to yourself right about now, "C'mon, who does that in this day and age?"

Believe me when I tell you that you'd be shocked to find out that this elemental function of creating a lasting relationship is being ignored or put on the backburner far more often than you'd think.

You should be striving to write thank-you letters that make people happier than before they gave you a gift. Make them excited to give to you again.

Some thoughts to try:

- Don't write a business thank you; you know the message you write in a thank you to your little Aunt Fanny? Write that kind of thank you.

- Take the time to explain to your donor how his or her gift made even a little difference or a little impact in the life or lives of those you serve. Sometimes a bite-sized example is easier to understand and believe than saying, "Your gift moved mountains, caused the earth to shake, changed day to night."

- Invite your supporters to a free event, like a behind-the-scenes tour or a special conference call to hear about a possible new project.

- Be creative in your opening sentence. Don't say, "On behalf of" or "From the bottom of my heart." **Do use language like**, "What a great surprise this morning. I opened the mail and there was a gift from you," or "I've got to share this with you…"

- Try using photographs that show the results of the good work being done as a result of donor support.

- Do a simple video in which you say something like "Thank you for doing XYZ." Or how about a thank-you video starring the person featured in the appeal?

- Talk about a specific aspect of your program that will benefit from the gift the donor made. It will give them a sense of what you're doing with their money.

- Who else, besides yourself, could say thank you? The beneficiary? The board chair? Remember, they write it, but you send it. Or maybe a board member can send one as a follow-up to your thank you.

Repeat after me, **you can't ever thank a donor often enough!**

I want to give you a few snippets of thank you letters that do a great job of letting the donor know that he or she helped make a difference in someone's life.

The best way to do this is to be a storyteller.

- *Thanks to you, we have provided 25 children with*

a place to live, learn, and feel safe this year. Your donation will help purchase new computers for our kids over the next few months.

- *First and foremost, let me say thank you! Your recent gift of $200 says to me that you "get it." You understand just how valuable time spent being able to do cool stuff like riding a horse can be. And when you add in the therapeutic value to kids afflicted by _____, the value of your gift is nearly inestimable.*

- *Because of your gift, this week we were able to move an 80-year-old grandmother into a bright, well-furnished apartment in a neighborhood and community that puts the health and happiness of its older citizens first. Thank you!*

- *Because of you, we did it!*

THINGS TO REMEMBER:

- A prompt, well-thought out thank you is extremely important, especially when it comes to building relationships and getting the next gift.

- Think of your thank you strategically—it's the first step to getting the next gift when done well.

CHAPTER 22

MAKING FIRST-TIME DONORS WAIT IS LIKE PLAYING RUSSIAN ROULETTE

There's a reason why nonprofit experts thank donors within 48 hours of receiving a gift, especially a first-time gift. Your chances of receiving a second gift drop precipitously if donors, especially first-timers, have to wait much beyond that time frame.

We've sat back in disbelief on more than one occasion while visiting with a nonprofit as they tell us that it usually takes them as long as a month or more to "get around to" thanking their donors.

One well-known organization spends and spends and spends on new donor acquisition, often to the detriment of sustaining the donors they already have. We finally got them to understand that if they did a better job of making new donors feel sufficiently thanked and welcomed no more than 48-72 hours after a first gift had been received, they wouldn't need to be so dependent on one-time gifts year after year.

We instituted a retention and loyalty program with them

that made sure to communicate to new donors the impact their gift was having in real time. In addition, we helped them engage with their new donors by several contact touchpoints, such as updates on the latest news and invitations to low-key events.

We like to tell our clients that the secret to a great thank-you letter is that the donor actually feels better about his/her decision to give to you than they did before they made the gift.

Here are a couple of ways you can use your thank-you letter to make your donors, especially new donors, feel the same way:

- Offer something to do next like joining your email list to receive updates or extend an invitation to a free event or to visit your website.
- Thank them for being the kind of people who take action—not for their donation, but for being a doer, a "do-gooder giver" (I just made that one up, but it sounds kind of cool, don't you think?)

I'm often asked my opinion on the following:

Is it appropriate to ask for another gift in the thank you letter?

Most donors say they don't want to be asked for a second gift too quickly.

Since a donor who has given a second gift has a much higher retention rate, I always think the more judicious strategy is to do all you can to earn that next gift, rather than boldly asking for it when you thank a new donor.

Remember: donors, especially first-time donors who are looking to form relations with nonprofits, will often test you. They look on the first gift as dipping their toe in the ocean. This is of critical importance as far as retention and your pipeline of donors is concerned. These new donors don't necessarily need communication pieces that are extravagant or exaggerate impact. For example, they don't need to be told that their $15 gift saved the world from extinction. These "testers" simply want to know that you recognize and respect them as new donors and that their gift had meaning to you and, certainly, to the beneficiary.

> Don't let first timers become part of a never-ending cycle of ask, receive, repeat, with no reporting back to them. If you do, you'll lose them.

Penelope Burk, president of Cygnus Applied Research, Inc. suggests that there is an acknowledgement sweet spot of seven thanks for a gift. At first, that may sound like a lot, but we're not talking about seven thank you letters. It means seven points of communication or engagement with messaging that clearly expresses gratitude. These seven touches could be in the form of a video, newsletter, postcard, phone call, hand-written note, or impactful email. The important part of a thank-you strategy is incorporating different types of touches that engage the senses and provide variety as this new relationship begins.

It's been my experience that:

- *Most donors want to see how their first gift made a difference.*
- *A personalized letter is the preferred outreach method for most donors.*
- *About two to three months seems about the right amount of time to wait before asking for a second gift.*

My suggestion is that the above two to three months or so is about the right length of time from the first gift through **gratitude and stewardship** before asking again. Taking the time to cultivate the relationship will result in better donor retention and upgraded gifts.

I'd like to share with you a story from Kate Bousum, Director of Advancement at Child's Voice, where children with hearing loss are provided the skills and tools needed to learn to speak and listen. Here's Kate on the importance of **stewarding and expressing gratitude to donors:**

"In response to a mailed appeal, we had a generous family make a $10,000 gift. This past supporter had given before, but never anything significant. It was a surprise, and certainly wonderful to receive. We stewarded that family. We sent notes, artwork from those impacted by their gift, made thank you calls, and invited them to special events which they never attended. Though they didn't engage a lot, they were kind when we talked to them. This family didn't give again for six years. Then, in response to a mailed appeal, another $10,000 gift.

Stewardship matters. Letting people know how their financial support is being used, thanking them for their gift, long after it was it was directly implemented, matters. We continue to work to steward our donors. I hope you do, too!"

THINGS TO REMEMBER:

- Use your thank you note to engage donors, especially new ones, to do something.

- Ask your board members to help you make thank you phone calls or write thank you notes.

- Go out of your way to make a positive impression with new donors.

- An appropriate amount of gratitude and thoughtful stewardship should be practiced before asking for the next gift.

Donor Loyalty and Retention

Years ago, a friend of mine who was the planned giving director at the Chicago Civic Opera told me his best prospects for bequests weren't the major donors who sat in the best seats--they did their giving through their family foundations and corporations, and were likely to have complex estate plans focused on passing wealth to the next generation.

The best prospects were the long-time ticket holders who sat up in the balconies and seldom gave more than $100 to the annual fund. Their devotion to the organization and its mission was proven through attendance and interest. They were more likely to have relatively simple wills, leaving gifts to family members and causes they cherished.

I have seen this proven time and time again--at Brookfield Zoo, at an animal shelter, and now at Recovery International. We frequently receive bequests of $10,000 to $50,000 from people who have been long-time members or who have made modest annual fund donations. And then there are the big surprises--someone who died in 1999 left a trust for his daughter who passed away last year, and our organization was the recipient of the remainder of the trust upon her death. We received two hand-written checks totaling $1.5 million!

So, always value the donors who contribute modestly to the annual fund, respect their loyalty, build their interest, and make sure they know the basic language to include your organization in their wills. Perhaps, years from now, the seeds you plant today will bear fruit that will help your organization thrive and survive tough economic challenges.

Sandra K. Wilcoxon
Chief Executive Officer
Recovery International

CHAPTER 23

―

BUILDING TRUST AND LOYALTY: A DEEPER DIVE

I certainly agree with Sandra regarding the importance of the seeds you plant today continuing to bear fruit for years to come. This whole book is about creating a **process to develop an ongoing system that drives annual fund revenue.** The annual fund, if done properly, will give you major gift and planned giving prospects for years to come. **The next step in the process is Donor Retention and Loyalty.** Let's talk about how to do it right.

Prior to COVID-19, Sue and I attended a fundraising event as guests. While there, we made a personal gift, our first to this organization. The organization sent back two separate email receipts within a few days. After about a week, we got a far-from engaging tax receipt in the mail—almost identical to many, many that we've gotten from other organizations for years.

If this organization had put even a tiny bit of thought and imagination into what they sent us they very well may have received a second gift. Sadly, there was no attempt at a personal connection.

All they would have had to do was acknowledge our

presence at their event and at least a bit of a connection would have been made. Something like this:

"Thanks so much for attending our event. I was thrilled to be able to meet you and your wife and I'm very grateful that you're now a part of the important work we do. Thanks again for your support!"

Those words would have been enough to confirm that they actually knew and cared about the time and money Sue and I invested. Would there have been a little more effort involved? Yes, a little. **But remember this: it's the extra effort that distinguishes your organization from others and connects you to your donor.**

For the most part, Mr. or Ms. Donor tend to give to the same organization for about five or six years if you've been successful in getting that all-important second gift. The startling truth is that **precious few donors give a second gift and even fewer still ever become loyal donors.** When asked for help with donor retention, I ask a simple question:

What's your plan to retain them? "Oh, it's in my head, not on paper" is not an acceptable answer.

I can hear many of you right now thinking to yourselves, why doesn't Ron just come right out and give us his plan to solve the puzzle that is donor retention.

So here is a list of items that should be included in your donor retention plan:

- Appeals
- Surprises

- Thank you notes
- E-Newsletters
- Newsletters
- Phone-a-thons
- Thank-a-thons
- Volunteer opportunities
- Videos
- Invitations
- Social Media Communications

I know this much: the donor retention plans we've put into place at many organizations work when there is a laser focus and importance placed on being treated as true partners in the work you do, not as a means to an end—the money; but as an integral force behind the work you do.

If you're looking to maximize donor retention, and why wouldn't you be, the most important thing is to <u>try to create donors who are loyal to your cause.</u> A loyal donor is one who has a personal commitment to your work. That's very much different from a donor who simply gives several times.

I'm talking here about people you want to walk the walk with you because they believe so deeply in your mission and have capacity. Creating loyal donors will keep your organization thriving. These donors will spread the word to others for you—a benefit that can't be overestimated.

Specifically, you can help cultivate loyal donors, donors who trust you and your organization, by being transparent

with them about what you're doing with their money. It really is as simple as that.

When people give their hard-earned money, they want, expect, and deserve to know what happens when it gets to you. I assume you agree that's not asking too much.

Maintaining consistent, compelling communications with your donors increases your credibility as an organization.

A couple of suggestions:

1. *Be specific by breaking down big, abstract fundraising goals into smaller ones that will be easy for your donors to understand.* For example, if you're a social service organization that feeds the hungry and you need $500,000 in annual support, break that figure down by explaining that it's going to cost about $500 per year to feed x number of hungry people. Can you see how the smaller number is easier to comprehend? And when you frame donor support in terms of making a difference in the lives of individuals, they'll feel more connected to what you're trying to get done.

2. *Go a little further.* If you have a designer on staff, try creating charts and graphs to illustrate how you are using the support of your donors. You don't need to give donors a penny-by-penny breakdown. People will appreciate having a broad idea of how their support is being used. Image of a simple chart or fundraising diagram.

3. *Use emotion.* Remember, most donors let their hearts dictate their support. Don't rely solely on statistics. Tell specific, impactful stories that make your donors feel something. Do this in your thank-you notes, newsletters, impact reports, blogs, and other content. The combination of graphics and testimonials will help you create an emotional bond with your audience while also appealing to their logic.

Here's something to discuss with your staff, post on bulletin boards around and in your office, and declare in clear language that everyone at your organization will understand—**your nonprofit needs donors much, much more than they'll ever need you. If you don't believe this, go one year without doing any fundraising. That means no annual fund, no capital campaign, nothing. See what condition your organization will be in then. Heck, try it for six months—if you dare.** Everyone at your nonprofit needs to understand and buy into these words.

Here's what you need to focus on when it comes to donor retention:

- Figure out what is really important to your donors and talk to them about those things.
- Concentrate on those donors who have the most value and show them (prove to them) how much you love, respect, care for, and treasure their support. This is Job #1—everyday.
- Provide your donors with proof every day that they are true difference-makers.

- Invest in retaining the donors you have. Invest in a plan.
- The future rather than the past-what upcoming opportunities are available for your donors and prospects to be difference makers?

As an example of this last bullet point, let me share with you a couple of excerpts of an appeal from Dutchess Community College Foundation:

Dear Sam,

I'd like to share a heartwarming story about three amazing alumni who I had the pleasure of meeting this past spring.

I recently received a call from a young man named Mike. He was interested in creating a scholarship along with his two friends and fellow alums, Adam and Joe. All three had continued on for their bachelor's degrees in engineering.

The three returned to Dutchess County to begin their careers, and wanted to recognize the positive impact Dutchess Community College had on their lives by creating a scholarship for future engineering students at DCC. They were even able to receive matching funds from their employer.

They were excited about the prospect of paying it forward.

These three young men were pulling together to help others pursue a higher education.

Deserving DCC students count on people like Mike, Adam, Joe—and you—to help them achieve their academic goals. You, *too, can establish your own scholarship-but until then, will you please make a gift of $100 to help The DCC Foundation support scholarship initiatives?*

Diana Pollard, Executive Director

Dutchess Community College Foundation

What a great example of helping donors see the opportunities and the impact giving can have!

In short, **your ability to keep donors with you longer is the key to your success.** You can be successful at this. If you're a leader at your nonprofit organization and are looking to throw money at something–throw it at this. Seriously.

I'm often asked to suggest a tactic that can be used to help with donor retention. Here's an old standby for you: *surprise your donors with a thank you on the anniversary of their first gift to your organization or in celebration of an event that their support made happen.*

I know you've heard this before, but it certainly can't be said enough–it costs more to find a new donor than it does to keep the donor you already have invested in continuing to support your work.

If you understand some of the reasons why donors turn their backs on organizations they previously supported, you can come up with strategies and tactics to keep them engaged.

Donors lose interest in your mission for various reasons:

- Because they don't think you need them anymore,
- Because they don't get enough feedback from you on how their money was used,

- Because they don't remember having supported you,
- Because they don't feel sufficiently thanked,
- Because another organization has convinced them that they're more deserving,
- Because they can no longer afford to make a gift.

These are some, but certainly not all of the reasons donors stop giving. Knowing these, can you see that there are many possible steps that can be taken to stem the tide of poor donor retention? There's a common "something" in these reasons—almost everyone is completely within your organization's power to control (with the exception of the last bulleted item).

Try **building a profile** of your high value donors and using it to identify prospective new donors. What you want to be sure to do is to differentiate the characteristics of lesser-value donors from those of higher-value individuals.

Being knowledgeable about how your supporters feel about your work and the role they'd like to play is the beginning of any effort to improve donor retention.

If you think this whole donor retention hoopla is exaggerated, ask yourself why the for-profit world invests so much time and revenue in knowing as much as they can about their customers and, as a result, enjoy a close to 90 percent retention rate.[1]

In case you're wondering, nationally, nonprofit retention is nearly 50 points less than in the for-profit arena. Nonprofits should hide their heads in shame when this issue comes up.

Suggestion: Take a survey of your employees in the near future. Ask them to describe your organization's mission. Then do the same with your donors. While you and your employees may believe that your nonprofit does x, y, and z, your donors may say that they believe you do a, b, and c.

The point of this kind of survey would be to make sure that there's alignment between what you do and what your donors' perception of what you do really is. If you find that the results come out very differently, you should be trying to accomplish the things donors believe you're striving to do. After all, that's what they're giving to.

In short, when you can match what your donors know and believe about you with what you actually do—that's when **your donor retention will skyrocket.**

I've also found the following to be true: *If you are successful at getting donors to give a third gift, there is a very good likelihood that you will extend their giving to your organization by three to four additional years beyond the time that the third gift is received.*

The caveat to this "giving business" goes back to **creating a *"habit of giving"*** within your constituents, because the longer you can extend the life of your relationship with your donors, the greater the chances are that they'll remain loyal and generous.

Here are practical tactics for retaining your donors:

1. Get your acknowledgement/thank you letter out within 48-72 hours.

2. Send an email or handwritten note to donors addressing the impact of the first gift.
3. Share a special video or photo of beneficiaries.
4. Tell them specifically what was done with their money.
5. Share three to five different communications, i.e., emails, newsletters, impact report, etc.
6. Explain why the work your organization does is important.
7. Send a welcome packet – Engage them!
8. Ask them to volunteer.
9. Ask them to share social media posts.
10. Invite them for a tour.
11. Ask for a second gift within 60 -90 days.
12. Ask for a small increase.
13. Ask for a specific need.

Here's a beautiful story from my friend, Eric Wilkie, chief development officer at the Anne Carlsen Center in Fargo, North Dakota, that explains the importance of communicating with your donors.

My first year being a director of development, we were fundraising for the annual fund at a small private k-12 school. The school had never raised much more than $750,000 in a single year for the annual fund. They had a bold goal my first year of $1 million. Well, we did all the basics. First, we set the goal and shared with all of our supporters, parents, alumni, board members, community members, and churches. Then we started communicating the goal with our direct mail stories, always emphasizing the impact the dollars had on the mission. Next, we made all the appropriate visits and contacts, searching out the best prospects and made direct asks to those we identified. We were trying to do the right work.

Like many schools, our fiscal year ended on June 30th and we had had a pretty good year. We sat at around $900,000 by June 15th. I felt like I had made every phone call, knocked on every door, and told the story to as many people as physically possible. I was exhausted, but it looked like we would be short of our goal. Then, with only one week left in the fiscal year, John and Marie showed up.

A little background…Marie was a graduate of the school and she and her husband were wonderful supporters. Long before my time, they had made some very nice gifts to the school. When I started, I made an effort to get to know them. On my first outing with them I started asking questions. I think it made the board chair and president, who were along for that original visit, a little uncomfortable, but I thought it was important to hear from them rather than just sharing everything we were doing. A friend always told me that God gave us two ears and one mouth for a reason. One question in particular I asked was "What are your dreams for the school?" Marie and John pondered for a moment, then shared that they wanted to see the school go on, impacting more students each year and that we stay true to the mission that they both so valued. I asked the questions because we were trying to do the work the right way.

Back to the end of the fiscal year...John and Marie showed up in late June. With school out, they actually had to walk around our building to find an open door. We almost missed them but they found a door and made their way up to my office. The first thing they asked (because we had shared so often throughout the year about our progress) was how our annual fund drive was going. I shared with them that we had had an amazing year and we had come so close, but we were thankful for all the new supporters and the future looked bright with enrollment and giving up for the year. John and Marie just smiled...reached out a hand with an envelope and said "I think you'll hit your goal".

That envelope contained a $250,000 gift, not only taking us to our goal, but surpassing it! We were elated and John and Marie could not have been more pleased to make that impactful gift. We would go on to raise $1 million dollars each year for the next two years, increased and made our goal of $1.1 million the fourth year. Because of the momentum in the annual fund we were able to undertake a major campaign to reduce the school's debt by raising another $6 million. I've heard the annual fund referred to as the soil for your organization. If you have a good base of soil you can grow almost anything!

John and Marie are a great reminder that if you do the right work and do the work the right way, you will get the right results.

Eric Wilkie, CFRE
Chief Development Officer
Anne Carlsen Center

THINGS TO REMEMBER:

- Donor retention is key to a successful annual fund.
- Your organization needs donors more than they need you.
- Invest in a donor retention plan.
- You must work on retention and acquisition at the same time.

1 Bloomberg, 2017 March 22

CHAPTER 24

ARE PRINTED NEWSLETTERS WORTH IT?

Newsletters, it turns out, just like appeal letters, will bring you more support—if they're well done and focused on the donor, not organizational impact.

One of our clients didn't want to do away with the print version of her newsletter. The board, however, had a different idea. What the board wasn't taking into consideration was the fact that many of their constituents didn't use emails. Also, the organization used the printed newsletters as handouts at speaking engagements.

A compromise was struck and our client, in lieu of doing away with the print version altogether, agreed to cut the number of pages from 12 to 8. She asked Rescigno's to help her write a more donor-focused newsletter that would be easier for people to read. In other words, like with appeals, a newsletter that is easy to skim.

For the first time in their history, a return envelope for donations was included. I'm happy to say that the new, more donor-focused, less-expensive version, doubled the donations previously received.

I've always thought of a print newsletter as a very unique way to provide hard evidence of the work your organization does. It's a great way to tell your donors many things. Here are a few examples:

- What their support is helping to accomplish; To educate your donors;
- To explain your mission;
- To deepen relationships;
- To inspire trust and more loyalty.

What else does a print version of your newsletter accomplish?

- It will reach people who you don't have an email address for;
- It will appeal to those who are more comfortable giving in response to print;
- Because many organizations are doing only enewsletters, it will stand out as special.
- It becomes an attractive addition to your coffee-table library for others to enjoy.

Here's something to think about: *while there is a case to be made for enewsletters, many people have suggested recently that enewsletters are often something they mean to get to but never do. Sound familiar? Think of the things that you've been meaning to look at in your inbox right now that have been sitting there for days, weeks, months. Out of sight = maybe out of mind.*

One of the factors that many don't consider when doing their newsletter is the way it's put together and mailed. There are pros and cons to the question of doing a self-mailer or enclosing your newsletter into an envelope. The envelope is a little more costly, that's true. However, doing it this way does allow you to add an insert more efficiently and put a teaser on the outside of the envelope.

What's in a "well-done" newsletter?

Among other things:

- Information that isn't boring; facts and statistics are boring unless they support an emotional story
- Information that is short and to the point
- Information that allows donors to feel good about their support
- Information about what donors are making possible; not your staff, not your board—donors
- Information that is donor-focused, i.e., "you," not we; "your," not our or we or us
- Information and pictures and fewer words

Your newsletter should be one of your very best fundraising tools. Have you ever thought about your newsletter as a fundraising tool instead of as a reporting device? Your newsletter is another opportunity to **show your donors the impact of their giving. That's what donors want to know about and what causes them to feel a stronger bond with you.**

Here are the four principles we emphasize when it comes to **newsletters that build donor loyalty:**

1. The difference that the donor is making. Just like with your appeals, make the donor the star. When you consider putting anything into your newsletter, ask yourself, "Does this information show the donor that his/her participation mattered?" If the answer is no, get rid of it.

2. Remember to stress, Because of you! Remind donors often how critical they are to your work.

3. I'm often asked if there should be an "ask" in a nonprofit newsletter. My answer is no, there doesn't need to be an ask, but that doesn't mean that you have to completely avoid asking for gifts. Remember, donors want to know that you need them. If there is a financial reason, be clear and direct. Ask for their help.

4. Tell a story. Let it include these:

    (a) a description of what the problem or need was;

    (b) what your organization did to solve the problem;

    (c) The happy ending or resolution to the problem.

<u>And remember to always show that the donor is the one who made the difference -- who allowed the organization to get things done.</u> If your fundraising budget doesn't allow for a department newsletter, then you should ask for a few pages in the marketing department's newsletter and make sure your donors are on that list.

THINGS TO REMEMBER:

- Just like with your appeals, you should think of your newsletter as a fundraising tool, not just a way to get a "communication piece" out.

- Use your newsletter as a way to build donor loyalty.

CHAPTER 25

DONOR COMMUNICATION PLAN FOR BUILDING LOYALTY AND RETENTION

As I mentioned earlier, I often ask nonprofit prospects if I can see their donor communication plan. When I'm told, "Well, it's not in writing…it's in my head" I can imagine a bus rumbling down the street heading straight for the person who has the plan in his or her head. Rest in peace!

The reason you need a plan or strategy, really, is quite simple.

The quickest and most efficient way to develop a consistent source of support is to develop relationships. Why is a relationship so important? Why don't donors understand the work your organization does and give again and again without you having to go the proverbial extra mile to "connect" with them?

If you've ever had a serious romantic relationship you probably understand the role "connecting" or engaging plays. This does take time and effort. There's no doubt about that.

It's impossible to overestimate the importance of having

loyal donors that love what you do and who will sustain your work for several years at least.

Whether you work with annual giving donors or major giving, there are a few elements of a donor communication plan that will help to build a sense of loyalty and trust.

What we're talking about here is providing your donors with meaningful information that is educational and interesting in-between appeals.

> When you give donors information they value, you're building up their familiarity with your cause and gaining their trust. Over time, this improves their loyalty to you.

We've created donor communication plans for nonprofits who really believed they were doing a good job of communicating with their donors. In reality though, if the plan doesn't complement fundraising activities, it's not a very productive plan.

Tactics to Include in Your Donor Communication Plan

Think of the information you send after a donor makes a gift. The information should include a thank you letter, tax receipt, new donor welcome packet and/or phone call. Do you know what information gets sent to which donor and when? You should review your current materials and identify who gets what.

Also, take a look at what you send out on a monthly basis.

You should think about these as touchpoints that help your organization stay in touch with your donors through meaningful updates. I'm talking about newsletters, gratitude reports, handwritten notes, phone calls, etc. Really, the list is limited only by your imagination and budget.

The important thing to remember is to space out what you're sending so these messages don't overlap with your appeals. Also, segment your donors and create more touches to those who donate more or are considered your best prospects. So, your plan should include a funnel for those that give below $99, $100 – $249, $250 - $499, etc.

Once you understand your communication funnels, then make sure that what you're sending is the right piece to the right audience.

Below is an example of a communication funnel that could be used for donors of a certain level:

- You receive a gift from a recurring donor.
- You generate a donor-centered acknowledgement NOW.
- Within 48-72 hours, send a personalized, donor-friendly thank you via direct mail or email...do you know your donor's preference?
- Within the next two weeks, send a postcard featuring an impact story as you connect the dots between your organization and the donor, not your organization as the difference maker.
- Within three months, send a story of another donor that talks about why he/she gives.

- In six months, send an update on an ongoing project the donor has supported, if applicable.
- Just before the one-year anniversary of the first gift, send a story that shows impact and demonstrates the impact an additional gift of support will have.

Additional guidelines:
- Communicate with your donors at least once every three months.
- Communicate personally based on new vs. current donors who have increased their gifts.
- Thank your donors often.
- Send newsletters that are donor friendly. Make it about them, not your accomplishments.
- Invite donors to special events both large and small.
- Invite your donors to take part in special campaigns like Giving Tuesday.
- Feature special donors in your newsletter or other communication pieces.

A word about multiple channels of communication: Have you ever stopped to consider the fact that donors who are connected to you through multi-channel communications give significantly more than donors connected by only one channel? It's true, and their retention and conversion rates are better, too.

THINGS TO REMEMBER:

- Your donor communication plan should be tailored to segments of donors, not generic.
- Create donor communication funnels for each segment.

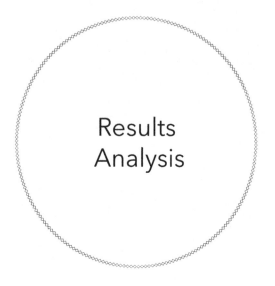

Results
Analysis

CHAPTER 26

ANALYZING IS THE KEY TO GROWTH

Think about how exciting it is when money starts arriving after you've sent out an appeal. You count it all up after a certain period of time, and, if you've done a good job of telling an impactful story, you're probably gratified with the results.

Don't stop there. In order to understand how your appeal performed, you should analyze each specific mailing six to eight weeks after your mail drop date. After each mailing, you should complete an analysis form with the total amount of gifts and actual dollar amounts raised. Every segment should be clearly identified, which will allow you to see each segment's response and average gift rate.

And don't forget to count all those gifts that came in online during the six to eight weeks after your mail dropped. If those people received the direct mail piece, you can be sure they are going online because of it. Count those as a specific segment.

In your report, you should identify response rate, cost per piece, average gift, percentage of upgrades and downgrades, along with analyzing how donors are using the ask strings on the reply card.

At the end of the year, you should do a comprehensive analysis identifying the following:

- Donor Retention Rates - How does your rate compare to the national average and what are you are doing to increase year over year?
- New Donor Retention Rates - How many first-time donors gave a second gift? Are you doing enough to engage them to give a second gift?
- Percentage of Upgrades- How many donors are increasing their gifts? Are you always asking for an increased gift? Are you asking for an increase often enough?
- Percentage of Downgrades- Why are donors decreasing their giving? Have you asked for an increase? How can you get them back to giving at their usual rate or higher?
- Cost of donor renewals vs. cost of acquisition
- Giving History- Can you identify trends in donor giving? Can you identify major gift prospects? Can you identify planned giving prospects?

Once the information is collected, put together an analysis on each appeal's performance, which will then help you make more informative decisions on future appeals.

Now we have completed THE PROCESS-DRIVEN ANNUAL FUND

DISCOVERY – DATA WEALTH SCREENING, ANALYSIS, DONOR

PROFILING – PLANNING AND MESSAGING – ACKNOWLEDGMENT – DONOR RETENTION- RESULTS ANALYSIS

Once you complete this process you must continue it year after year and each year. If you do, you will watch your Annual Fund program grow and prosper no matter the size of your organization.

THINGS TO REMEMBER

- Each year there should be a comprehensive analysis done of your annual fund program.
- Without analysis there can be no clear path for improving the annual fund.

CHAPTER 27

WHAT ABOUT ONLINE? "DIRECT MAIL IS SOOOOOO EXPENSIVE!"

Be at ease! If your organization isn't exactly killing it with online giving, join the party. Online giving is increasing, it's just doing so more slowly than many had predicted. Where we see online growth really taking off is with #GivingTuesday, which is the first Tuesday after Thanksgiving. Due especially to mobile devices, millions have been given during this time. Recently I read that 50 percent more donors respond to direct mail when receiving the same call-to-action across multiple channels.1

Having said that, success online probably doesn't happen if there is a lack of investment.

Sound familiar?

That's right. The same factors that contribute to a lack of success in non-digital spaces apply digitally. That is, factors that can be laid at the feet of a lack of staff, skill, and budget.

To be successful online, the right staff with the right skill set has to be in place. Along with that, the ability to offer meaningful content to the right audience at the right time via the right channels is vital.

Unfortunately, this goes awry when a nonprofit doesn't have the ability or staff in place to measure, analyze, and improve their online fundraising efforts.

Speaking specifically about emails, nonprofits are sending out more and more emails to prospects and donors, yet getting fewer responses. At least that's the feedback we've been getting.

As best as I can tell, it's because these emails have not been segmented to speak to the right audience, at the right time, with the right message.

I'm often asked, "What's our competition doing?"

In case you're wondering, I never tell. I'll speak in generalities, but never specifics.

I can tell you this. We see that **one of the areas where our nonprofit clients are finding success is in pre and post emails before and after their solicitation appeal has gone out.** You should try it. It works.

About a week or two before you send the actual hard copy appeal, a primer email that alerts the recipient to be looking for the story of someone who benefitted from the donor's support is a great way to get the donor thinking about donating again.

Likewise, send another email a week or two after the appeal goes out, reminding donors that by now they should have received the appeal about so and so. In that, you can say you're hoping that they can make their gift if they haven't already done so. If you're looking for a nice, gentle way of asking a second time, now you have one.

The bottom line here is that emails are a good way to communicate with your donors and prospects. Generally speaking, however, they have not proven to be a good vehicle for appeals.

THINGS TO REMEMBER:

- Sending an email before and after your direct mail solicitation will increase your response rates.
- Direct mail solicitations are still the number one source of finding new donors.

1 Mobile Cause.com, 2015 October 14

Chapter 28

ASTOUND AND AMAZE YOUR BOARD WITH YOUR INFORMED INSIGHTS

We work with many boards on how they can fulfill their fundraising responsibilities. You'd be surprised (or maybe you wouldn't) at what they don't know. Often, they were allowed to become board members without being trained or having their responsibilities explained to them in terms of expectations that go along with any perceived prestige.

After all, raising money is very often not an area that many board members have any experience with. However, many do have business skills that apply directly. Having a clear strategy, thinking long term, understanding the budget, checking out the competition, exploring the data, knowing your customers, and taking a leadership role are just some of the ways they can put their business skills to use as board members.

If you really want to form a connection with your board members (and amaze and astound them at the same time), answer these questions that they ask all the time.

- *What's the plan?* Talk to them about past fundraising efforts–those that have worked and those that haven't-- and future plans so that they can see that there is a strategy. We've noticed that just the act of taking the time to explain the strategy helps them to understand the pressures you face and can make the relationship between you and them less adversarial. **Presidents can be very helpful if they take on the leadership role of talking to their board members about this.** It will make them feel special and that they have access to him.

- *What condition is the budget in?* Explain that no matter how well thought out your strategy is, without the proper investment, finding success will be very difficult to achieve. Give an overview of how the budget has changed over the last few years. Discuss areas in the budget where you feel you are over or under-invested. Ask for their input.

- *What are the strengths and weaknesses of the foundation/development office?* Judging the performance of your fundraising efforts is very difficult if no parameters exist as to what's good and what isn't. A clear understanding of what other organizations are achieving as you discuss strengths and weaknesses is also helpful.

- *What do your donors look like?* Hopefully, you can provide the necessary data to reveal things like the numbers of donors, how they were recruited, and at what level they are giving. If you're not readily able to provide them with that information, maybe there needs to be some resources put into data management.

- *Are we doing a good job of keeping our donors?* As already noted, donor retention is a big problem. Three out of every four new donors to an organization never make a second gift. That's not a good thing at all. Discuss your donor stewardship efforts with your board. **Caring for donors cannot be overestimated. It should be the core of your future fundraising plans.**

- *What can we do to help?* Explain that fundraising is a team sport and that it's so much easier to deliver positive results when you feel like you have the support of everyone behind you.

Boards! What can I say? How about you can't live with them and you can't live without them!

In our presentations, we stress that board members play an absolutely vital role in creating and/or maintaining a culture of philanthropy at any nonprofit organization.

THINGS TO REMEMBER:

- Educating your board about what your office is trying to accomplish (and how they can help) will pay big dividends. The more you communicate your plan, the more they'll buy in.
- Be creative in coming up with new ways for board members to help you fundraise.

CHAPTER 29

———

THE FUTURE OF DIRECT MAIL FUNDRAISING — HERE'S HOW WE SEE IT

While there's no denying the surge in popularity of all things digital, direct mail fundraising is still a very significant driver for nonprofit organizations, especially when it comes to the The Process-Driven Annual Fund.

Is direct mail fundraising here to stay? For the foreseeable future, it is. Of that, there can be no doubt.

By way of review, I've put together some trends that I think you'll find interesting:

Trend #1- Your Story

To a greater degree than ever before, you have to know your audience and be able to tell them a story that describes your brand - not what you do, but why you do it. Again, I'll use the example I used earlier of the maintenance man who understands why he does what he does and is able to succinctly explain it to visitors at the hospital where he works. When asked by a prospect what he did, he replied, "I help heal people by keeping this hospital as clean as possible." His story revolves around the reason the hospital exists—to heal people. Very powerful stuff!

The same thing goes for direct mail. Be a storyteller. Follow the process, know your audience, and tell them stories and listen for stories that you can retell that reflect your mission. They don't have to be long or particularly involved. They do, however, have to be emotionally "involving" if you're hoping for a gift.

You should know what type of story your audience responds best to and be feeding them that kind of story on a regular basis (segmentation). No matter the type of story you tell, though, **every story you tell should make your donor fall in love with your organization all over again.**

Trend #2 - Use Variable Data Printing

Segmentation pays off. Period. The deeper you dig, the better the reward will be. And there's plenty of evidence showing that donors want and need personalized communications.

Be honest, do you really think any of your direct mail or email recipients are moved at all by a solicitation that's obviously been sent to hundreds, if not thousands, of other people?

You need to meet donors at their level and provide them the experience, inspiration, and the connection they are looking for from your organization.

Overwhelmingly, the trend is to provide the right message at the right time in the right way. **One size does not fit all.**

You should create donor personas that describe, among other things, donor likes and dislikes, their preferences, passions, motivations, demographics, and, of course, giving history.

Here's the thing. Aligning your fundraising efforts with your donor's personas will greatly reduce the chances of your communications being ignored.

In short, to segment effectively, you should know the answers to these questions:

- How often does the donor want to receive communications from your organization?
- Does the donor have a preferred channel for receiving your communications?
- What kinds of communications does your donor want to receive?
- Which programs or causes is the donor most interested in?
- What "generation demographic" do your donors fall into?
- What is the donor's connection to your organization?
- How much does the donor donate annually?
- How loyal is the donor?

Trend #3 - Working to Create a Culture of Philanthropy Will Make Your Job Easier

Creating the culture is everyone's job. That means development staff, support staff, program people, board members, and last, but not least, leadership. In fact, **the culture** must start with, and trickle down from, leadership.

What does a philanthropic culture mean? **It means putting donors smack dab in the middle of everything you do. It means you stop making them the means to an end—the money.**

This culture also means that you treat your donors with so much respect, love, and inclusivity that they feel like a vital part of your mission.

And that's the point of philanthropy. **Does your organization think and treat donors as a money machine or a central part of the solution to the problems you confront on a daily basis?**

And that's what we mean when we say that organizations that don't have a culture of philanthropy may be doing well (or not), **but there's little doubt that hundreds of thousands of dollars are being left on the table when donors are not treated as part of the answer and not looked upon and thought of as equal partners in your mission.**

There are so many more lessons we've learned over our time working with many great nonprofit organizations, and I'm sure there are many more that we'll be learning in the years ahead.

Sue and I and the rest of the team at Rescigno's are looking forward to what these next few years have in store for all of us who are engaged in the noble work of nonprofit fundraising.

There is one final lesson we've learned since we began in 1992 and it's that you, our current and future clients, remain central to what we do. If you walk into our office, the first thing you'll see is a statement of our philosophy, which says:

Customers are the most important visitors on our premises. Customers are not dependent on us-we are dependent on them. Customers are not outsiders in our business-they are a part of it. We are not doing them a favor by servicing them... they are doing us a favor by giving us an opportunity to do so."

Hmmm, that pretty much sums up the way you should think about your donors, doesn't it?

As the years have gone by, the need for The Process-Driven Annual Fund has become more and more clear to me.

If, like too many nonprofit organizations we encounter, you don't have a plan (in writing) in place, now is the time to do so.

Your annual fund should serve as the foundation for all of your fundraising activities. It's where you compile a base of donors who you involve, inform, and, hopefully, connect and engage with.

If your annual fund is successful, your nonprofit can go onto higher-level fundraising initiatives because you've established a steady flow of income for the basics—your programs, services, and activities.

You've probably heard this many times before, but I'd like to repeat it here. *There is an art and a science to fundraising.*

I think this is particularly true as far as the annual fund and direct mail fundraising are concerned. There are scientific features of the work you do that prove you're doing things the way they should be done. And that kind of verification is helpful.

But, when all is said and done, successful annual fund fundraising is much more "art" than it is anything else.

The best annual fund appeals are as close as one can get to face-to-face fundraising and there's certainly an art to that, isn't there?

If you use the content described in this book, I'm certain you'll be better able to engage your donors in more emotional, heartfelt ways, and that the end result will be both stronger relationships with your donors that endure the test of time and much more revenue than you ever thought possible.

Just as important, you'll discover donors who have a real desire to help your cause. Whoever thought that the annual fund and direct mail could do all that?

About The Author

A colleague, after reading Ron's blogs and newsletters, once said, "He is a person I would like to have a glass of wine or a beer with. His literary voice is approachable, friendly, and has a Chicago south side feel to it. His style of writing is both unique and inviting." A great compliment when you consider that Ron doesn't drink and isn't originally from the south side of Chicago. He has written this book for fundraising professionals responsible for raising annual fund money. Ron has helped nonprofit organizations grow their base of support for over 28 years. Known as Rescigno's copyediting guru, he works with clients to create appeal letters that pass the 'donor-focused' test. In his book, he describes the Process he has developed for annual fund success.

For more information, blogs and to download free templates and resources please visit **ronrescigno.com**, **rescignos.com** or email him at **ron@rescignos.com**.